Keynote

3

Workbook

Wisniewska

NATIONAL GEOGRAPHIC LEARNING | CENGAGE Learning

Australia • Brazil • Mexico • Singapore • United Kingdom • United States

NATIONAL GEOGRAPHIC LEARNING | CENGAGE Learning

Keynote Workbook 3
Ingrid Wisniewska

Publisher: Andrew Robinson
Executive Editor: Sean Bermingham
Senior Development Editor: Derek Mackrell
Development Editor: Christopher Street
Director of Global Marketing: Ian Martin
Senior Product Marketing Manager: Caitlin Thomas
IP Analyst: Kyle Cooper
IP Project Manager: Carissa Poweleit
Media Researcher: Leila Hishmeh
Senior Director of Production: Michael Burggren
Senior Production Controller: Tan Jin Hock
Manufacturing Planner: Mary Beth Hennebury
Compositor: MPS North America LLC
Cover/Text Design: Brenda Carmichael
Cover Photo: Cyclists reflected in Main-Danube Canal near Nurnberg: © Gerd Ludwig/ National Geographic Creative

© 2017 National Geographic Learning, a part of Cengage Learning

ALL RIGHTS RESERVED. No part of this work covered by the copyright herein may be reproduced or distributed in any form or by any means, except as permitted by U.S. copyright law, without the prior written permission of the copyright owner.

"National Geographic," "National Geographic Society" and the Yellow Border Design are registered trademarks of the National Geographic Society
® Marcas Registradas

For product information and technology assistance, contact us at
Cengage Learning Customer & Sales Support, 1-800-354-9706

For permission to use material from this text or product, submit all requests online at **cengage.com/permissions**
Further permissions questions can be emailed to
permissionrequest@cengage.com

ISBN-13: 978-1-337-10416-6

National Geographic Learning
20 Channel Center Street
Boston, MA 02210
USA

Cengage Learning is a leading provider of customized learning solutions with office locations around the globe, including Singapore, the United Kingdom, Australia, Mexico, Brazil, and Japan.

Cengage Learning products are represented in Canada by Nelson Education, Ltd.

Visit National Geographic Learning online at **NGL.cengage.com**
Visit our corporate website at **www.cengage.com**

Printed in China
Print Number: 03   Print Year: 2023

Contents

Scope and Sequence

UNIT		LESSON A	LESSON B
	TITLE	**VOCABULARY** **LISTENING**	**LANGUAGE FOCUS** **LISTENING FOCUS**
1	**Making a Difference**	Giving help Inspiring dreams	Discussing ways to contribute Reduced speech
2	**Trends**	Describing trends Analyzing trends	Future trends Intonation
3	**Improving Lives**	Talking about healthcare The health check of the future?	Discussing cause and effect Stress for emphasis
4	**Designing the Web**	Describing website features Designing websites	Making comparisons Linking
5	**Community Builders**	Making communities better Creating green spaces	Using the passive voice Word stress: *can* and *can't*
6	**Clear Communication**	Using communication collocations Communication styles	Describing types of communicators Intonation when agreeing and disagreeing
7	**Identity**	Describing identity Multicultural experiences	Discussing current events Unstressed words
8	**Transportation Solutions**	Describing modes of transportation An unusual commute	Making travel predictions Contraction of *will*
9	**New Words**	Describing language Collecting words	Describing word trends Pronunciation of *used to*
10	**Understanding Emotions**	Describing feelings Dealing with emotions	Discussing EQ and jobs Contraction of *would* or *had*
11	**Leaders and Thinkers**	Doing business Starting a business	Talking about what makes a good leader Linking sounds
12	**Well-being**	Describing health and well-being What your brain does when you sleep	Discussing facts about sleep *Will* and *would*

LESSON C VOCABULARY BUILDING	LESSON D TED PLAYLIST	LESSON E WRITING
Prefix *min-*	How to step up in the face of disaster Cheap effective shelter for disaster relief Emergency shelters made from paper	Desribing an inspiring person
Collocations with *advantage*	How yard bombing grew into a worldwide movement The tribes we lead Meet the founder of the blog revolution	Describing a product or service
Collocations with *pressure*	A warm embrace that saves lives Printing a human kidney A test for Parkinson's with a phone call	A letter to a health tech company
Word group *attach*	Human-centered design A delightful way to teach kids about computers Simplicity sells	Writing a review
Suffix *-ant*	Building a park in the sky A park underneath the hustle and bustle of New York City A guerilla gardener in South Central LA	Making a suggestion
Collocations with *span*	CERN's supercollider The most mysterious star in the universe How we'll find life on other planets	Giving an explanation
Suffixes *-ant*, *-ancy*, and *-ance*	Don't ask me where I'm from, ask me where I'm a local Embracing otherness, embracing myself The danger of a single story	Writing a reflection
Collocations with *charge*	Excuse me, may I rent your car? Uber's plan to get more people into fewer cars New York's streets? Not so mean any more	Describing an invention
Forming verbs from adjectives	Go ahead, make up new words Don't insist on English Txtng is killing language. JK!!!	Making an argument
Collocations with *combine*, *comfort*, *companion*, *permission*, and *privacy*	A look inside the brain in real time How we read each other's minds Robots that "show emotion"	Expressing an opinion
Collocations with *action*	How to manage for collective creativity How to run a company with (almost) no rules Why good leaders make you feel safe	Describing your business style
Word group *satisfy*	The power of time off The happy secret to better work Got a meeting? Take a walk	Making suggestions

1 Making a Difference

1A

VOCABULARY Giving help

A Complete the paragraph using the correct form of the words or phrases in the box.

be there for them	encourage	help out
make an impact	take care of	inspiring

My social studies teacher in sixth grade was a very [1] ________________ person. He made us believe we could make a difference. He told us that even small acts of kindness could [2] ________________ on the people around us. He [3] ________________ us to find ways to help people in the community. We could offer to [4] ________________ around the neighborhood. One way I used to help my neighbors was to [5] ________________ their pets when they were away. Small acts of kindness like these show others that we will [6] ________________ if they ever need help.

B Answer the questions using your own words.

1 When was the last time someone helped you out?

____

2 How do you try to make a difference to the people around you?

____

LISTENING Inspiring dreams

A ▶ 1.1 Listen to a podcast. What is it about?

a Three charities you should volunteer to help.

b How to create a volunteer program.

c How to choose the best volunteer program.

B ▶ 1.1 Listen again. Which pieces of advice are mentioned in the talk? Check [✓] all that apply.

1 ☐ give volunteers paid time off

2 ☐ create volunteer teams

3 ☐ make a list of charities that need help

4 ☐ force employees to volunteer

5 ☐ show appreciation to volunteers

COMMUNICATION Talking about helping others

A Circle the best response for each question.

1 Do your classmates often ask you for help?

a Yeah, sometimes. I help them with their homework.

b Thanks, I can manage on my own.

2 Have you helped any of your neighbors recently?

a No way! As much as possible, I try not to ask anyone for help.

b Well, I watered Mrs. Green's plants while she was on vacation last week.

3 When was the last time you helped a stranger?

a Um, I guess it was a couple of weeks ago.

b Sure. What's the problem?

B Answer the questions using your own words.

1 When was the last time you helped someone out?

____

2 What did you do for them?

____

3 How did they feel about it?

____

1B

LANGUAGE FOCUS Discussing ways to contribute

A Complete the conversation. Number the sentences (**1–8**) in the correct order.

a ______ Sounds like you had a good time. Maybe I should volunteer too.

b __5__ Wow! That must have been really hard work.

c __1__ Have you volunteered before?

d ______ Well, I worked with other volunteers and we painted all the children's rooms.

e ______ What did you do there?

f ______ I guess it was. But I enjoyed it a lot and the kids were really happy.

g ______ Yes, I have. I helped out an orphanage once.

h ______ You should. It can be a lot of fun, and it's a chance to make a difference.

B Circle the correct word to complete each sentence.

1 Did you (**volunteer** / **volunteered**) last year?

2 I've (**signed** / **sign**) up as a volunteer at the animal shelter.

3 How do you (**helped** / **help**) other people in your daily life?

4 Volunteering (**has changed** / **was changing**) my outlook on life. I am now more grateful for all I have.

5 I developed an app to help abuse victims when I (**was working** / **am working**) at the children's home.

C Find and correct the three mistakes in the paragraph below.

I often volunteer to help out at charity fund-raisers. I've been to three events last year, and I've been to two so far this year. The last event I went to was for a children's charity. In total, the event was raising over $100,000! It's so nice to feel that I played a part in that. I also get to meet a lot of new people, and I've made so many new friends. I even meet my husband at a charity event three years ago.

LISTENING FOCUS Reduced speech

A ▶ 1.2 We often make words and phrases shorter when we speak. This is called reduced speech. Listen to and repeat the examples.

What **do you** do as a volunteer? → **Whaddaya** do as a volunteer?

What **did you** do as a volunteer? → **Whadidja** do as a volunteer?

B ▶ 1.3 Listen to each question. Circle the word you hear.

1 What kind of work (**do** / **did**) you do?

2 How (**do** / **did**) you get to work?

3 Who (**do** / **did**) you ask for help?

4 What (**do** / **did**) you like about being a volunteer?

C ▶ 1.4 Listen to each question. Circle the best response.

1 **a** I work in an orphanage.
  b I worked in an orphanage.

2 **a** Yes, I really enjoyed working there.
  b Yes, I really enjoy working there.

3 **a** I help them with their studies.
  b I helped them with their studies.

4 **a** Yes, I do.
  b Yes, I did.

1C

READING

Read the passage and answer the questions.

Hugh Evans (left) speaks at the Global Citizen Festival, New York.

As a 14-year-old, Australian Hugh Evans joined a volunteer program and traveled to some of the poorest parts of Manila in the Philippines. The experience made such an impact on him that he decided to devote his life to ending extreme poverty.

Evans's goal is to make a difference in the world. As a college student, he started the Oaktree Foundation, which raised millions of dollars for schools and education programs in developing countries. After that, he led a campaign to persuade the Australian government to double its foreign aid. The campaign organized a huge concert—the *Make Poverty History* concert. The aim of the free concert was not to raise money but to raise awareness of world poverty and to persuade world financial leaders to increase aid to developing countries.

Evans continues to be passionate about raising awareness of world poverty—now using the power of the Internet. In 2008, he founded the Global Poverty Project to campaign for government and business leaders to take more action against poverty. The organization engages and educates people about world poverty through an online community of volunteers, and is committed to ending world poverty by 2020.

In 2011, the Global Poverty Project organized the Global Citizen Festival in Central Park in New York City. To get tickets, people had to sign up on the website and get points by taking actions toward ending world poverty (for example, by watching a video, signing an online petition, writing a letter, or donating money to a charity).

Sixty thousand people attended the festival and helped to raise $1.3 billion for projects to fight poverty. The festival inspired thousands of people to help end world poverty. Every person in the audience was committed to making a difference. And that is the start of long-term sustainable change.

A What is the passage mainly about? Circle the best answer.

a a man who donated a huge amount of money to charity

b a man who spent his life as a volunteer in poor countries

c a man who engaged people to take action against poverty

B Circle **T** for true, **F** for false, or **NG** for not given.

1	Hugh Evans was inspired by a visit to the Philippines.	**T**	**F**	**NG**
2	Evans worked as a volunteer at a school in Manila.	**T**	**F**	**NG**
3	Evans was a student when he founded the Oaktree Foundation.	**T**	**F**	**NG**
4	The main aim of the Make Poverty History concert was to raise money.	**T**	**F**	**NG**
5	There was no admission fee for the Make Poverty History concert.	**T**	**F**	**NG**
6	The Global Citizen Festival raised $1.3 billion.	**T**	**F**	**NG**

LISTENING

A ▶ **1.5** Listen. What is the talk mainly about?

a the problems faced by charities in developing countries

b one charity that provides sustainable help to poor communities

c charities that help poor communities in developing countries

B ▶ **1.5** Listen again. What kind of aid does this charity give? Check [✓] all that are mentioned in the talk.

1 money ☐ **2** food ☐ **3** water ☐ **4** animals ☐ **5** training ☐

C **CRITICAL THINKING** Use the information (**a–e**) to complete the Venn diagram. Look back at the reading on page 9 if necessary.

a founded in the 21st century

b aims to convince world leaders to take action to end poverty

c focuses on long-term sustainable change

d founded by a farmer

e works actively to educate people

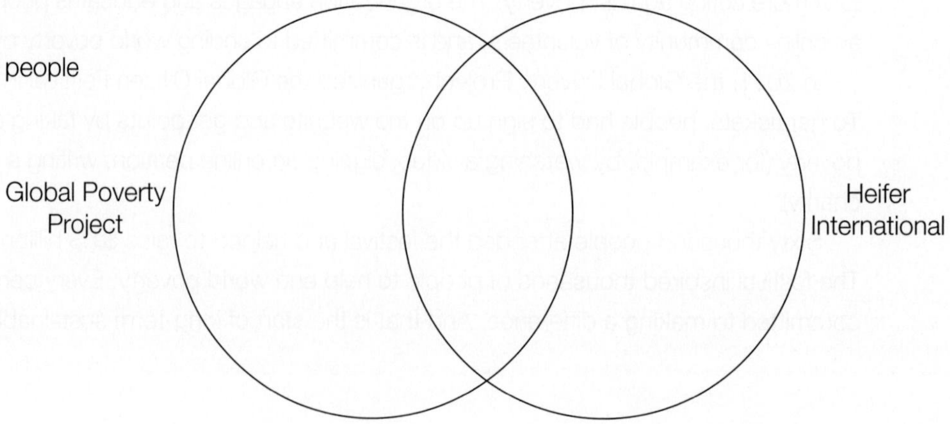

VOCABULARY BUILDING

A Choose a word from the box to replace each word in **bold**.

committed	devote	insignificant
minimize	passionate	

1 Small actions can seem **unimportant** but they can have a big impact. ____________

2 Many people are **very enthusiastic** about making a difference. ____________

3 Some people are **determined** to help end poverty. ____________

4 It's a good idea to **reduce** the amount of energy we use. ____________

5 It's inspiring to see people who **completely give** their lives to helping others. ____________

B The prefix *min-* means *small* or *less*, for example *minimize*. Match the words to the correct definition.

1 minimum (*n.*) ○ ○ **a** lesser or secondary in importance

2 miniature (*adj.*) ○ ○ **b** the least possible amount of something

3 minor (*adj.*) ○ ○ **c** smaller than others of the same kind

C Complete the sentences using the words in the box.

miniature	minimum	minor

1 She had a very ____________ role in the play.

2 The ____________ sum to donate is ten dollars.

3 The toy house was filled with ____________ chairs and tables.

Aid is delivered in Aceh after the Indian Ocean Earthquake and Tsunami in 2004.

TEDTALKS

1D

TED PLAYLIST

Residents of Fukuchiyama, Japan, are rescued from severe flooding.

HOW TO STEP UP IN THE FACE OF DISASTER

When a tornado hit their hometown in the United States, sisters Caitria and Morgan O'Neill—just 20 and 24 at the time—realized there was a desperate need for someone with the skills to organize people and the supplies to help. So they took charge and are now teaching others how to do the same with their website Recovers.org.

CHEAP, EFFECTIVE SHELTER FOR DISASTER RELIEF

After a disaster, people need shelter immediately, but it takes a long time to build temporary housing. Michael McDaniel designed housing that is inexpensive, easy to transport, and easy to set up. But he couldn't find anyone to build it. In the end, he decided to start his own company. In this talk, he shows us his Exo Reaction Housing Solution.

EMERGENCY SHELTERS MADE FROM PAPER

Imagine a house made from cardboard paper tubes. Prize-winning architect Shigeru Ban has designed museums and other important buildings. But he wanted to use architecture to help ordinary people. So he started building houses from materials such as cardboard tubes for people affected by natural disasters.

A What is each talk about? Match the topic to the speaker.

1 buildings made from simple materials	○	○	**a** Caitria and Morgan O'Neill
2 organizing help after a disaster	○	○	**b** Michael McDaniel
3 quick and easy homes for the homeless	○	○	**c** Shigeru Ban

B Which speakers most likely said the following? Circle the correct answer.

1 "We spent five weeks rebuilding the church. It was meant to stay there for three years, but actually it stayed there 10 years."

a Caitria and Morgan O'Neill **b** Michael McDaniel **c** Shigeru Ban

2 "We just started answering questions and making decisions because someone—anyone—had to. And why not me?"

a Caitria and Morgan O'Neill **b** Michael McDaniel **c** Shigeru Ban

3 "They can actually stack together so we get extremely efficient transportation and storage out of them."

a Caitria and Morgan O'Neill **b** Michael McDaniel **c** Shigeru Ban

C Decide which talk you most want to watch. Watch it online at www.ted.com.

1E

WRITING Describing an inspiring person

A Read the sample paragraph about a person who's made an impact on someone's life.

Write one paragraph. Start by describing someone who inspired you.

Someone who has made a big difference in my life is my English teacher in high school. She was very sensitive and kind. I didn't like school very much because I didn't have any friends. I think she noticed that I was sad. So she encouraged me to read and gave me a list of books to read during the summer vacation. I learned to love reading, a habit that has stayed with me all my life. Now I am in college studying English literature! I haven't forgotten my high school teacher, and whenever I have time, I volunteer at our local public library to read stories with children. I hope to help them learn to love reading, too.

Use some new words from this unit.

Then say how you felt before they helped you.

Describe how they inspired you.

Say how this has changed your life.

B Think about someone you know who has made a difference in your life. Answer the questions to plan your paragraph.

1 Who was the person who inspired you? What was special about them?

2 How did you feel before they helped you?

3 What did they inspire you to do?

4 What kind of impact has this had on your life?

C Now write your paragraph. Then complete the checklist below.

- ☐ Did you use correct spelling and punctuation?
- ☐ Did you use verb tenses correctly?
- ☐ Did you use some new words from this unit?
- ☐ Did you give an example of how your life has changed?

2 Trends

2A

VOCABULARY Describing trends

A Complete the information. Circle the correct words.

In recent years, improvements in technology have led to [1] (**growing** / **more and more**) jobs being carried out by machines rather than humans. According to a Pew Research report, almost half of all current jobs in the United States could disappear by 2025 as a result of [2] (**widespread** / **shrinking**) automation.

Travel agencies, for example, have [3] (**decreased** / **gotten worse**) in number as more and more people choose to book their vacations online. When you go to a bank, it is now quite [4] (**common** / **increasing**) to carry out your transactions through a machine rather than interacting with a human.

Are any jobs still safe? Experts suggest that jobs requiring creativity and social skills are the safest. The number of hairdressers and beauty salons, for example, is still [5] (**growing** / **more and more**).

B Answer the questions using your own words.

1 In the future, do you think the number of jobs done by machines will **increase**? Why or why not?

____

____

2 Do you think robot teachers will ever become **common**? Why or why not?

____

____

3 Do you think society will **improve** if more jobs are done by machines? Why or why not?

____

____

LISTENING Analyzing trends

A ▶ **2.1** Listen. Circle the correct answer.

1 What is the talk mainly about?

a why blogs are popular **b** the history of blogs

2 According to the talk, which of the following is true about blogs?

a They are still popular today. **b** They are starting to become less popular.

B ▶ **2.1** Listen again. Circle **T** for true, **F** for false, or **NG** for not given.

1 Blogging became popular in the early 1990s.	**T**	**F**	**NG**
2 The word *blog* was first used in the 1990s.	**T**	**F**	**NG**
3 The word *blog* is a short form of the word *blogger*.	**T**	**F**	**NG**
4 Music blogs are more common than technology blogs.	**T**	**F**	**NG**
5 Big companies spend millions of dollars developing blogs.	**T**	**F**	**NG**
6 Today, there are around 150 million blogs on the Internet.	**T**	**F**	**NG**

COMMUNICATION Talking about trends

A Complete the conversation. Number the sentences (**1–6**) in the correct order.

a ______ Well, I use an app that gives me recommendations.
b ______ I agree. How do you decide which movies to watch? There are so many online.
c __1__ Do you prefer watching movies online or buying DVDs?
d ______ Good idea! How about movie blogs, do you read those too?
e ______ That's easy, definitely online. DVDs take up too much space.
f ______ Oh, yes! I follow several blogs to find out about new movies.

B Answer the questions using your own words.

1 Do you prefer watching movies online or buying DVDs? Why?

____

____

2 How do you decide what movies to watch or what music to listen to?

____

____

2B

LANGUAGE FOCUS Future trends

A Circle the best option to complete each sentence.

1 In fifty years, there (**will** / **won't**) be printed textbooks in the classroom. Students will all have tablets.
2 Robots (**will** / **won't**) be a common household item. Everyone will have one.
3 People (**are** / **aren't**) going to be more connected to the Internet. Everything we own will be linked to it.
4 Shopping online (**is** / **isn't**) going to be the most popular way to shop. There will be fewer stores.

B Circle the best response.

1 I'm going to go for a jog this evening.

a I'm sorry I couldn't come along. **b** That's great! Can I join you?

2 I don't think I'll be able to join you for dinner.

a Oh no, shall we meet another time? **b** It's OK. We had a great time.

3 I think home robots will become very popular in the next five years.

a I don't think it will be so soon. **b** It was a great invention that benefited mankind.

4 Are you going to Maria's birthday party?

a No, I couldn't make it. **b** Yes. I'm bringing my cousin, too.

C Make predictions about the future using the words provided and *will* or *going to*.

1 artificial intelligence / become / more widespread / five years

____

2 humans / live / on other planets / 20 years from now

____

3 time travel / not be possible / in ten years time

____

4 cars and trains / not change very much / in the next five years

____

LISTENING FOCUS Intonation

A ▶ **2.2** We use intonation to stress words that contrast with each other. Notice how the speaker's voice rises on the first choice and falls on the second. Listen and repeat what you hear.

Do you think life in the future will be **better**, or **worse**?

Do you think robots will make life **easier**, or more **difficult**?

B ▶ **2.3** Read the questions. Underline the words that should be stressed. Then listen to check your answers.

1 Do you think people will have more free time, or less?

2 Will cities become larger, or smaller?

3 Do you think air travel will be faster, or just the same?

4 Will the world's population increase, or decrease?

C ▶ **2.3** Listen again. Draw arrows to show the intonation.

2C

READING

Read the passage and answer the questions.

1 Do you think you know a lot about the latest trends in fashion, music, and culture? Then you might be the right person for a job as a coolhunter!

2 In today's interconnected world, trends spread, and change, quicker than ever before. What's in fashion one week can become outdated the next. It's therefore vital for many companies to keep up to date with what's trending and make sure their products stay popular. This is where coolhunters earn their dollars.

3 A coolhunter's job is it to spot patterns and make predictions about what will become the next big thing. Most coolhunters work in the fields of fashion, design, or technology. Many of them also have their own blogs, where they identify current trends and post pictures of the latest fashion and design ideas.

4 But how does a coolhunter stay ahead of the game? Networking is important. Many coolhunters have a network of social, business, and online contacts. These could be influential bloggers or other trendsetters, such as magazine editors or key decision makers in other companies.

5 It's also important for coolhunters to observe the people around them. They need to take notice of people's clothing, accessories, and gadgets. They often spend time socializing, and are constantly looking for the coolest new places to hang out.

Aimee Song is a popular fashion and interior design blogger.

6 And of course, being active online is vital for any modern coolhunter. Spending time online, visiting websites, writing blogs, and engaging in social media networks are the most effective ways of finding out what's hot and what's not.

7 The number of people employed as coolhunters is expected to rise in the future. There are even universities that offer coolhunting courses. So if you're hunting for a cool new career, perhaps this is the one for you!

A Match the headings with the paragraphs.

1 People Watching	○	○	**a** Paragraph 3
2 Networking	○	○	**b** Paragraph 4
3 Having an Online Presence	○	○	**c** Paragraph 5
4 What is a Coolhunter?	○	○	**d** Paragraph 6

B Circle the best answers according to the information in the passage.

1 How are trends different nowadays?

a They change more rapidly. **b** They are started by younger people.

2 Which of these would be a good contact for a coolhunter?

a A famous sports person **b** The CEO of a technology company

3 How is the number of coolhunter jobs expected to change in the future?

a It's likely to rise. **b** It's likely to fall.

LISTENING

A ▶ **2.4** Listen. Check [✓] the influences on fashion trends that are mentioned in the talk.

☐ street styles ☐ famous designers ☐ friends

☐ fashion shows ☐ fashion bloggers ☐ celebrities

B ▶ **2.4** Listen again. Circle the best answers according to the information in the talk.

1 What is street style?

a fashion worn by ordinary people **b** the latest fashion for casual wear

2 Why is the fashion blogger Chiara Ferragni mentioned?

a because she made a lot of money from her fashion blog
b because she has a huge number of online followers

3 Why are some people becoming increasingly influenced by their friends' fashion ideas?

a because social media makes it easier to share pictures of fashion styles
b because our friends' opinions are becoming more important to us

4 What does the speaker say about trendsetters?

a There are fewer trendsetters than ever before.
b Due to social media, more people have the opportunity to be a trendsetter.

C **CRITICAL THINKING** Who do you think has a greater influence on trends: coolhunters or fashion bloggers? Give a reason to support your answer.

____

____

VOCABULARY BUILDING

A Complete the paragraph using the correct form of the words in the box.

analyze	emerge	relevant	take advantage of

Companies nowadays are [1] ________________ online resources to find out more about their customers. They have found that social media tools are becoming far more [2] ________________ to customer choices. For example, researchers who [3] ________________ a group of parents found that the majority of them regularly consulted social media sites before making purchases for their children. As a result, a new market is [4] ________________ for social media marketing experts.

B Read the paragraph below. Then choose the correct word to complete each sentence.

The Internet has changed customer shopping habits. Customers can now **take advantage of** the latest sales and promotions that are posted through websites, emails, online ads, and social media sites. Some businesses offer their customers the added convenience of shopping from the comfort of their own homes. This might seem like an **unfair advantage** over smaller businesses that are unable to offer the same services, but it is what consumers want and prefer—convenience at the click of a mouse. For these smaller businesses, it will definitely be **to their advantage** to harness the power of the Internet to reach more customers.

1 If you take advantage of something, you (**don't use** / **make good use of**) it.

2 If something is to your advantage, it will (**benefit** / **harm**) you.

3 If you have an unfair advantage, it's (**easier** / **harder**) for you to achieve something you would have had to work hard for.

2D

TED PLAYLIST

Yarn bombing of a bicycle in Cheshire, United Kingdom

HOW YARN BOMBING GREW INTO A WORLDWIDE MOVEMENT

Textile artist Magda Sayeg transforms urban landscapes into her own playground by decorating everyday objects with colorful knit works. These warm, fuzzy "yarn bombs" started small, but soon people took a liking to the craft and it spread across the world.

THE TRIBES WE LEAD

Seth Godin argues that the Internet has revived a human social unit from the distant past: tribes. He explains that the Internet gives us the power to find people who share the same ideas and values—giving ordinary people the power to lead and make a change. He encourages all of us to take advantage of this and start a tribe.

MEET THE FOUNDER OF THE BLOG REVOLUTION

The founding mother of the blog revolution, Movable Type's Mena Trott, talks about the early days of blogging, when she realized that giving regular people the power to share their lives online is the key to building a friendlier, more connected world.

A What is the theme of the playlist? Circle the best answer.

a new technology **b** trendsetting **c** being a leader

B Which speakers most likely said the following? Match the quote to the speaker.

1 "I reached all of these people, and I had tens of thousands of people reading about my life every day." ○ ○ **a** Magda Sayeg

2 "What I want you to do, it only takes 24 hours, is: create a movement." ○ ○ **b** Seth Godin

3 "And this was fun for me. It was really fun to take inanimate objects and have them come to life." ○ ○ **c** Mena Trott

C Decide which talk you most want to watch. Watch it online at www.ted.com.

2E

WRITING Describing a product or service

A Read the sample passage about a new product.

Write two paragraphs. In the first paragraph, describe your product or service.	Food scanners will become more <u>popular</u> in the future. People are paying more and more attention to what they eat, and this product will be able to instantly analyze the ingredients in food.	Use some new words from this unit.
In the second paragraph, describe the benefits of this product or service.	This will help people make informed decisions about their purchases. It will be especially beneficial for people who suffer from food allergies. <u>Other useful applications</u> of this product could be to analyze how many calories are in the food. This will benefit people who need to reduce their calorie intake or those who want to maintain a healthy diet.	Say who it will be useful for. Describe some other applications.

B Think about an idea for a new product or service. Answer the questions to plan your paragraph.

1 What is the product or service?

2 Who will this product or service be good for?

3 How will people benefit from it?

4 What possible applications could there be?

C Now write your paragraph. Then complete the checklist below.

- ☐ Did you use correct spelling and punctuation?
- ☐ Did you use some new words from this unit?
- ☐ Did you explain how it is used?
- ☐ Did you describe how it will help people?

3 Improving Lives

3A

VOCABULARY Talking about healthcare

A Complete the sentences using the words in the box.

motivate	suffers from	treatment	wearable

1 Smartwatches and fitness trackers are examples of ______________ technology.

2 I joined a support group to ______________ me on my weight loss journey.

3 My brother ______________ depression—there are days when he won't even leave his room.

4 Scientists have come up with a new ______________ for baldness in both men and women.

B Answer the questions using your own words.

1 Do you know someone who is a caregiver? What do they do?

____

2 Do you have any elderly family members? What kinds of healthcare do they receive?

____

3 Do you monitor your health? What do you do?

____

4 If you could find the cure for a disease, which disease would you choose? Why?

____

LISTENING The health check of the future?

A ▶ 3.1 Listen. Circle the best answer.

1 What is the talk about?

a a new medical robot that has been developed

b the possibility that robots that will replace human doctors

c how robot doctors can read patients' emotions

2 This talk discusses robots that can ___.

a identify health problems

b perform surgery

c provide care at home

B ▶ 3.1 Listen again. Complete the table using information from the talk.

Advantages of medical robots	Disadvantages of medical robots
Robots can perform [1] ______________ tests on patients.	Robots do not include [3] ______________ and [4] ______________ factors in their diagnosis.
Doctors can spend more time specializing in illnesses that are more [2] ______________.	Robots can't provide counselling and emotional [5] ______________ to patients.

COMMUNICATION Talking about staying healthy

A Complete the conversation. Number the sentences (**1–6**) in the correct order.

a ______ Thanks! Well, I try to eat a healthy diet and keep active.

b ______ Hmmm… Maybe I'll join you one day.

c ______ Do you do a lot of exercise?

d __1__ Wow! You're looking great! What's your secret?

e ______ Yeah, I go running at least three times a week.

f ______ Sure! It'll be great to exercise together.

B Answer the questions using your own words.

1 How often do you exercise?

____

2 What kind of sport or exercise would you like to do more often?

____

3 How could you make your lifestyle more active?

____

3B

LANGUAGE FOCUS Discussing cause and effect

A Complete the sentences using the words in the box.

result	because	due	so

1 You should brush your teeth every day ______________ you don't get cavities.

2 As a ______________ of having better healthcare for expectant mothers, infant mortality has decreased.

3 Obesity is on the rise ______________ people are eating more junk food.

4 The hospital could not cope with the high volume of patients ______________ to a shortage of doctors.

B Circle the correct words to complete the information.

People now are able to live much longer [1] (**so** / **because of**) improvements in medical care. The rate of deaths [2] (**due to** / **because**) cancer and other illnesses has fallen [3] (**because** / **as a result of**) new drugs and better medical technology. Sadly however, the cost of this medical care makes it difficult for everyone to benefit from it.

In some countries, health insurance is paid for through taxes [4] (**so** / **because**) people don't have to worry about the cost of hospital or doctor visits. However, there are countries where health insurance is private and costs a lot of money. People often delay going to the doctor [5] (**so** / **as**) it is so expensive. In poorer countries, basic healthcare is not even available [6] (**because** / **because of**) there aren't sufficient resources.

C Match the two parts of each sentence.

1 You should cut down your smoking as	o	o	**a** they keep your heart healthy.
2 Obesity in children is often due to	o	o	**b** cancer patients are able to live longer.
3 He had a heart attack last year,	o	o	**c** fast food and a lack of exercise.
4 As a result of new drugs and treatments,	o	o	**d** it causes many health complications.
5 Healthy fats are good for you because	o	o	**e** so he's very careful with his diet.

LISTENING FOCUS Stress for emphasis

A ▶ **3.2** We often place extra stress on key words in a conversation. Listen to and repeat the examples.

1 **A:** When do you usually play tennis?
B: I usually play tennis on **Sundays**.

2 **A:** What do you usually do on Sundays?
B: I usually **play tennis** on Sundays.

B ▶ **3.3** Read the examples. Underline one word in the answer to each question that you think should be given extra stress. Listen and check your answers.

1 **A:** When are you having lunch with Daniel?
B: I'm having lunch with him tomorrow.

2 **A:** Who are you having lunch with tomorrow?
B: I'm having lunch with Daniel tomorrow.

3 **A:** Are you having dinner with Daniel tomorrow?
B: No. I'm having lunch with him tomorrow.

C ▶ **3.4** Listen to each question. Circle the best answer.

1 **a** I usually eat **fruit** for breakfast. **b** I usually eat fruit for **breakfast**.

2 **a** I go to the **gym** after work. **b** I go to the gym **after work**.

3 **a** My **father** bought me this watch. **b** My father bought me this **watch**.

4 **a** The **doctor** told me to rest. **b** The doctor told me to **rest**.

3C

READING

Read the passage and answer the questions.

1 Advances in medical technology are helping many people who have Parkinson's disease. While there is still no cure, new innovative devices are improving the quality of life for Parkinson's sufferers.

2 Parkinson's disease affects a person's muscles and their ability to move. It is caused by a problem with the nerve cells in the brain. There is an important chemical called dopamine, which helps send signals to different parts of the brain, telling it when to move parts of the body. However, people with Parkinson's don't produce enough dopamine. As a result, they can't send the correct signals to their arms or legs when they want to move.

3 The main symptom of Parkinson's is constant tremors or shaking of the arms and legs, so patients tend to move very slowly. They have difficulty balancing when they are standing or walking. They may also have trouble speaking and eating. Parkinson's is a progressive disease, which means it gradually gets worse, but this can take a number of years.

4 There are many different kinds of medication to treat Parkinson's. Although some have been successful in slowing down the disease, none are able to completely cure it. One problem that scientists face is monitoring how much medication is needed by each patient. This is where technology is important. New wearable devices detect tremors and classify them based on their intensity. The data is then sent to doctors, allowing them to track patients' reactions to different medication doses.

The devices worn by Parkinson's sufferers are worn on the wrist like a smartwatch.

5 There may be no cure for Parkinson's yet, but with new advancements in drugs and wearable technology, there is hope that patients can have a better quality of life.

A Match each paragraph to its main idea.

1 Paragraph 2 ○ ○ **a** a new way to help people with Parkinson's disease

2 Paragraph 3 ○ ○ **b** how Parkinson's disease affects a person's behavior

3 Paragraph 4 ○ ○ **c** what causes Parkinson's disease

B Circle **T** for true, **F** for false, or **NG** for not given.

1 People who smoke are more likely to get Parkinson's disease.	**T**	**F**	**NG**
2 Parkinson's disease affects the function of the brain.	**T**	**F**	**NG**
3 Parkinson's disease usually develops very rapidly.	**T**	**F**	**NG**
4 Parkinson's disease can affect someone's ability to talk.	**T**	**F**	**NG**
5 Parkinson's disease is becoming more common.	**T**	**F**	**NG**
6 Scientists have discovered a cure for Parkinson's disease.	**T**	**F**	**NG**
7 The device detects a tremor and measures its strength.	**T**	**F**	**NG**

LISTENING

A ▶ **3.5** Listen. What can the device in the talk do?

a prevent heart disease **b** measure weight loss **c** monitor your health

B ▶ **3.5** Listen again. Circle the correct answer.

1 What does this device look like?

a a smartwatch **b** a small bandage

2 What is it used for?

a to collect data from a person's body **b** to treat certain diseases

3 Which of these is true about the device?

a It can collect data from a person's sweat. **b** It can predict when a heart attack will happen.

C **CRITICAL THINKING** Use the information (**a–d**) to complete the Venn diagram. Look back at the reading on page 25 if necessary.

a It is a device you wear on your arm.

b Its sensor can detect shaking.

c Its sensor can detect your blood sugar level.

d It can send data to a doctor.

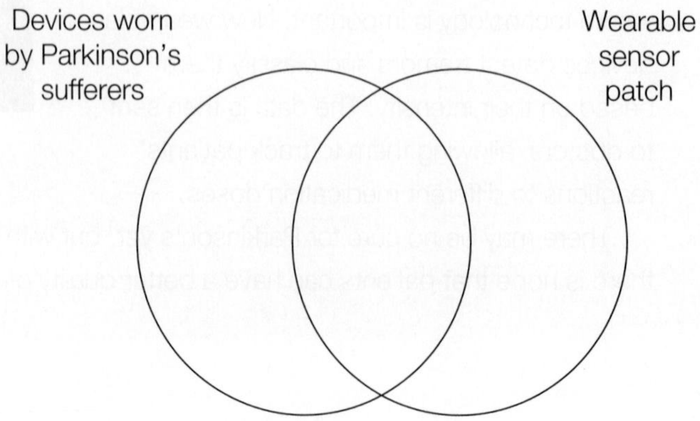

VOCABULARY BUILDING

A Choose a word from the box to replace each word in **bold**.

approach	behavior	constant	pressure	prevent

1 It may be possible to **stop** cancer by analyzing your DNA. ______________

2 Herbal medicine is an alternative healthcare **method**. ______________

3 There is a **never-ending** shortage of doctors and nurses in this hospital. ______________

4 The students were under a lot of **stress** to complete their assignment on time. ______________

5 Doctors monitor the **actions** of their patients to make sure there are no side effects to treatment. ______________

B Complete the sentences with the correct words.

blood pressure: *n.* the amount of force with which blood flows around the body
peer pressure: *n.* the social influence among people of the same group
under pressure: *ph.* to feel a lot of stress from somebody or something

1 He was ______________ to pass his final medical paper.

2 People with high ______________ are at risk of heart diseases.

3 Teenagers face a lot of ______________ from their schoolmates.

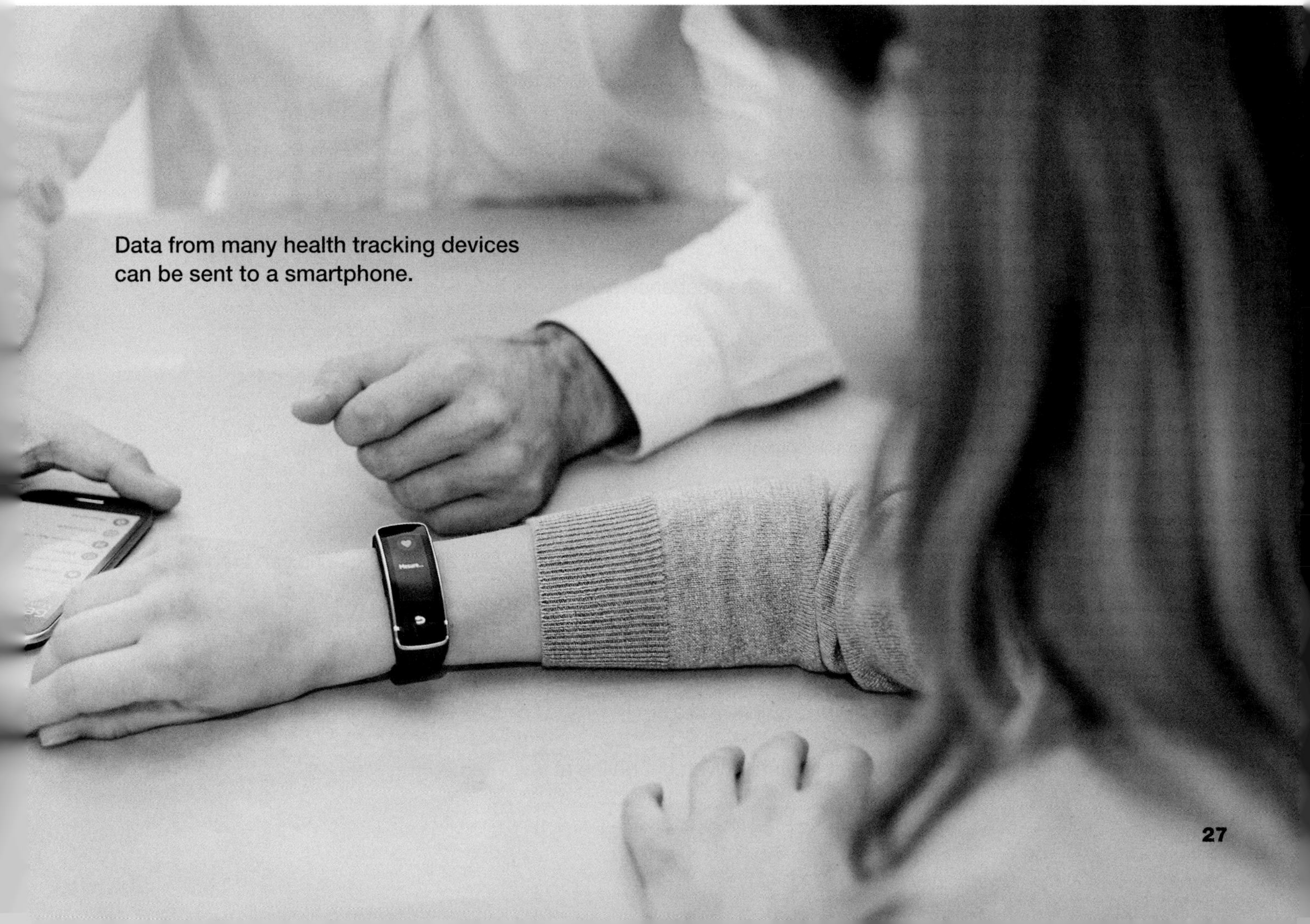

Data from many health tracking devices can be sent to a smartphone.

3D

TED PLAYLIST

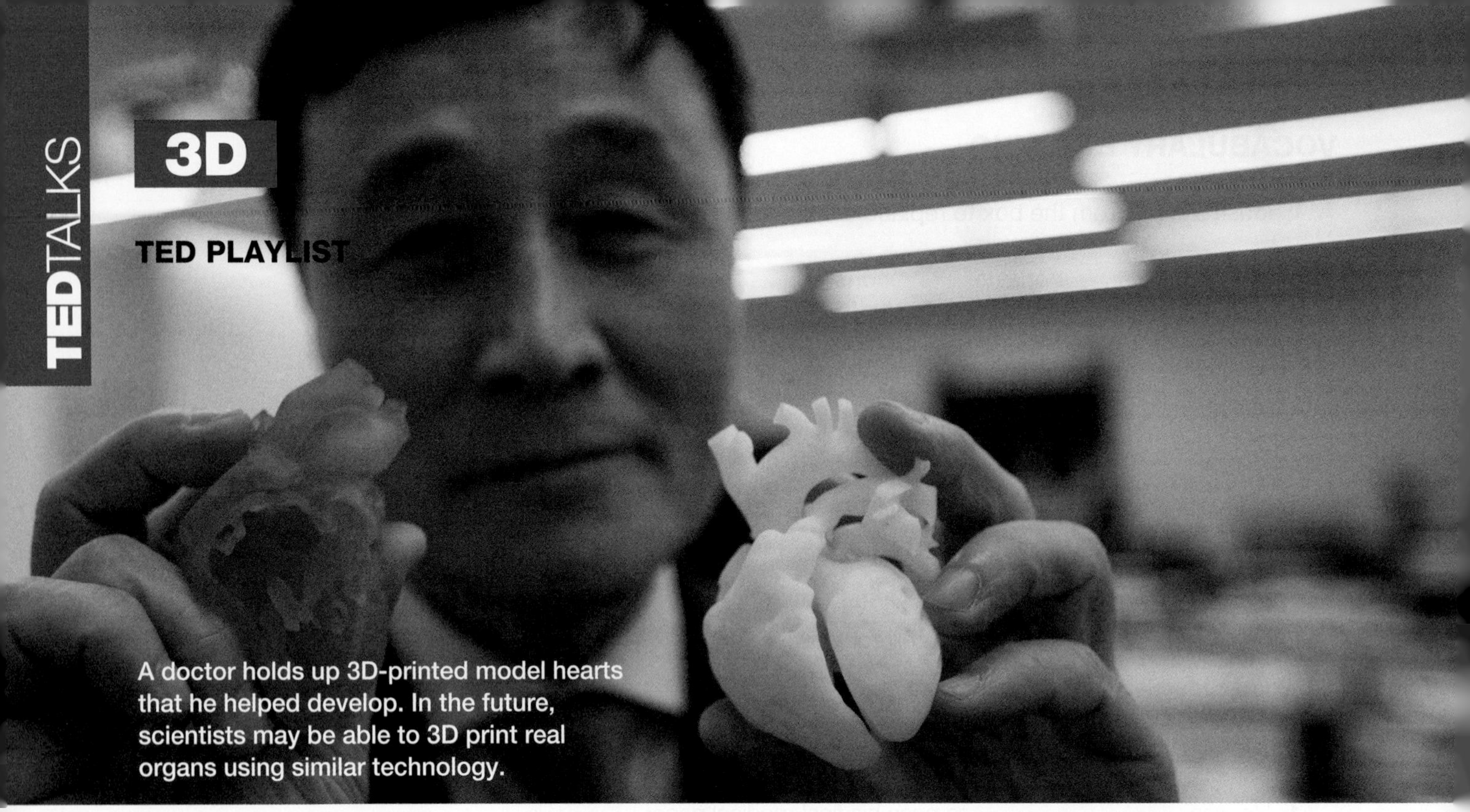

A doctor holds up 3D-printed model hearts that he helped develop. In the future, scientists may be able to 3D print real organs using similar technology.

A WARM EMBRACE THAT SAVES LIVES

Premature babies need special equipment to keep them warm. In some places, access to this equipment is limited, and millions of babies die each year. Jane Chen shows an invention that could keep these infants warm—a design that's safe, portable, and low-cost.

PRINTING A HUMAN KIDNEY

There are too few organ donors and thousands of people waiting for transplants. Surgeon Anthony Atala demonstrates an experiment that could someday solve the organ-donor problem: a 3D printer that uses living cells to produce a transplantable kidney.

A TEST FOR PARKINSON'S WITH A PHONE CALL

Parkinson's disease affects 6.3 million people worldwide but there's no way to detect it early. Max Little demonstrates a simple, cheap tool that is able to detect Parkinson's with 99 percent accuracy—in a 30-second phone call.

A What is the theme of the playlist? Circle the best answer.

a new healthcare technology **b** saving babies' lives **c** helping sufferers of disease

B Which speakers most likely said the following? Circle the correct answer.

1 "But what if patients could do this test at home? Now, that would actually save on a difficult trip to the clinic ... No expensive staff time required."

a Jane Chen **b** Anthony Atala **c** Max Little

2 "He looks like he's resting peacefully, but in fact he's struggling to stay alive because he can't regulate his own body temperature."

a Jane Chen **b** Anthony Atala **c** Max Little

3 "The problem is, not enough people agree to be donors upon their deaths."

a Jane Chen **b** Anthony Atala **c** Max Little

C Decide which talk you most want to watch. Watch it online at www.ted.com.

3E

WRITING A letter to a health tech company

A Read the sample letter about a technological solution for people who spend long hours at their desks.

Write two paragraphs. In the first paragraph, describe the health problem.

Dear Lifestyle Health Products,

People who sit at their desks for long periods of time are in danger of having more heart attacks and strokes than people who are active. They are often very focused on their work. As a result, they forget about the need to stand up and walk around from time to time.

Use words to express cause and result.

In the second paragraph, describe the benefits of this product.

One way to help them is to provide a wearable device for their wrist that monitors how long they have been sitting. Every half an hour, for example, it could beep to remind them to take a walk or do some exercises. This could be a very good way to help prevent heart attacks and strokes as well as obesity.

Sincerely,
Jane Robinson

Use some new words from this unit.

Conclude with an overall reason why your product will be helpful.

B Think about a group of people you know that might need some help with maintaining a healthy lifestyle. Write a short letter to a health tech company. Explain the problem and suggest a way to help them.

1 Describe the health problem.

2 What difficulties do these people have in their daily lives?

3 How could technology help to make their lives easier?

4 What are the possible applications for the solution you're offering?

C Now write your paragraph. Then complete the checklist below.

- ☐ Did you use the correct greeting and closing?
- ☐ Did you use correct spelling and punctuation?
- ☐ Did you use some new words from this unit?
- ☐ Did you describe how technology could help?

4 Designing the Web

4A

VOCABULARY Describing website features

A Match the definitions to the words on the right.

1 copy data from the Internet onto a computer	**a** browse
2 a design or symbol that represents a company	**b** button
3 an opinion of a product or website	**c** function
4 type in your password to enter a website	**d** log in
5 skim websites to find which ones are relevant	**e** logo
6 an icon that you can click to select a command	**f** review
7 a feature on a website such as "search" or "find"	**g** download

B Complete the information. Circle the correct words.

WE HAVE A NEW WEBSITE!

[1](**Log in** / **Review**) with your username and password and click the *Enter* [2](**logo** / **button**) to access our site. You can use the search [3](**function** / **logo**) to look for something you want, or [4](**browse** / **button**) our most popular news stories. Like something you see? Click on the [5](**download** / **review**) button and save it to your computer. Don't forget to head to our [6](**logo** / **review**) section. We want to know what you think about our new look. Your feedback is valuable to us!

LISTENING Designing websites

A ▶ 4.1 Listen. What aspects of website design does the speaker focus on?

☐ background ☐ headings ☐ images
☐ feedback ☐ icons ☐ logo

B ▶ 4.1 Listen again. How does the speaker suggest improving each one? Complete the sentences.

1 Use different fonts and ________________ for headings.

2 Change images once a ________________.

3 Use icons for the key ________________ on your website.

COMMUNICATION Talking about decisions

A Complete the conversation. Number the sentences (**1–7**) in the correct order.

a __1__ Is that a new camera?

b ______ Did you also check out the company's website?

c ______ Well, I compared reviews on several models on different websites.

d ______ How did you decide which one to get?

e ______ Yeah, I bought it online a few days ago.

f ______ Yes, I did. I watched some of their promotional videos.

g ______ Wow! All your research was worth it; it looks great.

B Answer the questions using your own words.

1 What gadget have you bought recently?

____

2 How did you decide which one to buy?

____

3 What advice would you give to people who want to buy this gadget?

____

4B

LANGUAGE FOCUS Making comparisons

A Complete the sentences. Use the words provided.

1 My new computer is much faster than my old one.

My old computer isn't as ________________ my new one. (fast)

2 This laptop is heavier than my tablet.

My tablet ________________ my laptop. (light)

3 These speakers aren't as good as those headphones.

These headphones ________________ those speakers. (good)

4 This camera is cheaper than all the other cameras.

This camera is ________________ one on the market. (cheap)

5 The features on this phone are different from the ones on my old phone.

The features on this phone aren't ________________ the ones on my old phone. (same)

B Complete the sentences using your own words.

1 ________________ are easier to carry than ________________.

2 ________________ isn't as expensive as ________________.

3 ________________ is almost the same as ________________, except for the price.

4 ________________ are much more expensive than ________________.

C Read the descriptions. Match the sentences with the correct items. Write **A**, **B**, or **C**.

Item	**A** 		**B** 		**C** 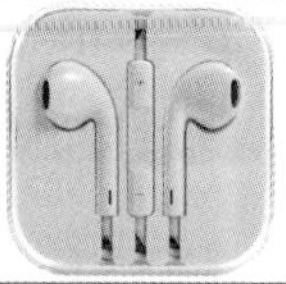	
Description	• $599 • Good for musicians • Quite heavy		• $179 • Good for home listening • Comfortable		• $59 • Good for sports • Lightweight	
Rating	**Overall**	**8.1**	**Overall**	**7.9**	**Overall**	**7.3**
	• Design	8.0	• Design	8.0	• Design	9.0
	• Features	7.0	• Features	7.5	• Features	7.0
	• Sound	9.5	• Sound	9.0	• Sound	6.0
	• Value	8.0	• Value	7.0	• Value	7.0

1 ________ They aren't the cheapest, but they have the best overall rating.

2 ________ They have the best features, and they are very comfortable to use.

3 ________ They have the best design, and they are good for jogging.

4 ________ They have the best sound quality, but they are pretty heavy.

5 ________ They are the cheapest, but they don't have very good sound quality.

LISTENING FOCUS Linking

A ▶ **4.2** Notice how a word ending with an /r/ sound links with the following vowel sound.

This computer is **faster and** easier to use than other models.

More and more are people going online to compare products.

B ▶ **4.3** Read the sentences below. Draw lines to show where the words are linked with an /r/ sound. Listen and check your answers.

1 The best feature is the sound quality.

2 There were other headphones in the review.

3 I'm looking for a cheap but stylish pair.

4 These headphones are good for outdoor use.

5 Each product received an overall score out of ten.

6 This one is more expensive than the others.

C ▶ **4.4** Listen to the conversation. Draw lines to show where the words are linked with an /r/ sound.

A: How's your new computer? Is it better than your old one?

B: It's faster and easier to use! I bought it online.

A: Really? Is it cheaper online?

B: Yes, it's more expensive to buy one in a store.

A: Wow! I never knew that. I should look online more often!

4C

READING

Read the passage and answer the questions.

Here are four easy dos and don'ts that will help you create a website that is fun and easy to use.

A Avoid cluttered pages. Use white space

Most people reading your page will just be scanning it to see if what they're looking for is on it. So it's important to target the information they need first and present it clearly. Don't fill your page with too much unwanted information.

B Include a search box

Many people have a very specific idea of what they are looking for. It might be a specific product or a name, for example, and they don't want to waste time scanning through all the pages to find it. A search function is essential as it will allow users to quickly find what they need.

C Don't ask users for too much information

It's useful to know who's visiting your site, but if you ask people too many questions, they'll just give up. No one wants to spend time completing long forms in order to get to the next page of your site. Even if you have a reason for collecting customer data, try to keep forms short and simple.

D Encourage feedback and questions

You can use your website to build a community of people who share the same interests. Encourage their participation by offering them a way to post comments and send you their questions. This is especially important for websites that sell products or services.

In conclusion, always keep your users' experience in mind and aim for clear and easy-to-use design features to make your website a winner!

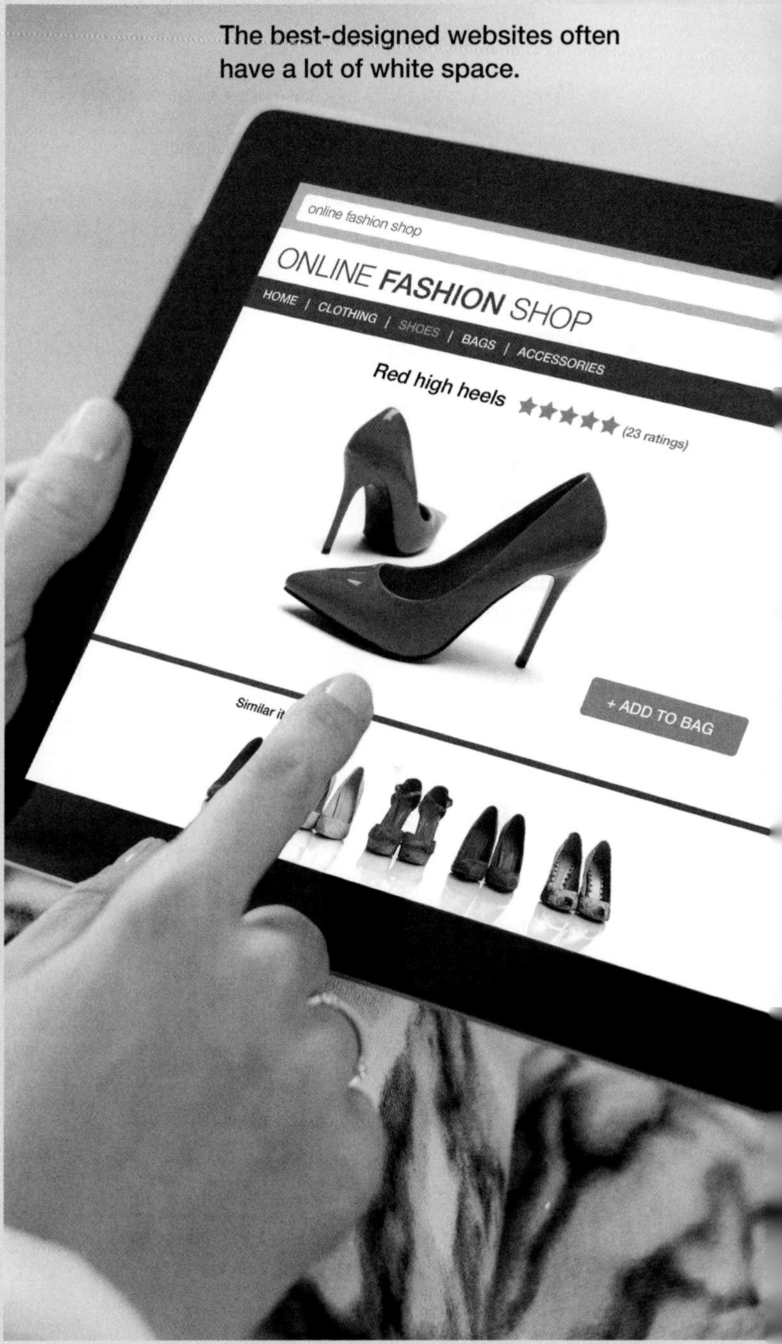

The best-designed websites often have a lot of white space.

A Choose the best title for the passage.

a Making Money Online **b** Four Great Websites **c** How to Make a Great Website

B Read the comments from a website's visitors. Which rule does each of the following break? Write the correct letter (**A**–**D**).

1 "There's no place for visitors to write their opinions." ____________

2 "The information given is too long and wordy." ____________

3 "There is too much text and too many pictures." ____________

4 "There's no way to ask for more information about the products." ____________

5 "Why do they need my email address?" ____________

6 "I had to scroll through every page to find what I was looking for." ____________

LISTENING

A ▶ **4.5** Listen. What are the two people talking about?

a Greg found a website where he bought some cheap headphones.

b Greg visited a website but didn't like the headphones.

c Greg went online to buy some headphones but didn't like the website.

B ▶ **4.5** Listen again. Did Greg have a positive or negative experience of the website features listed below? Circle **P** for positive or **N** for negative.

1 photos	**P**	**N**
2 descriptions	**P**	**N**
3 search box	**P**	**N**
4 navigation	**P**	**N**
5 order form	**P**	**N**
6 contact information	**P**	**N**
7 feedback form	**P**	**N**

C Which rules in the passage would be useful advice for the website Greg visited? Check [✓] all that apply.

a avoid cluttered pages, use white space ☐

b don't ask users for too much information ☐

c include a search box ☐

d encourage feedback and questions ☐

VOCABULARY BUILDING

A Complete the sentences using the words in the box.

attached to	encourage	impact	frustrating	spam

1 What new technology has had a high ________________ on your life?

2 Which tech device are you most ________________?

3 Isn't it ________________ to get so much junk mail every day?

4 Do you have a(n) ________________ blocker on your email?

5 Does your employer actively ________________ you to give feedback on your job?

B Read the definitions below. Then complete the sentences using the correct form of the words in **bold**.

attach: (*v.*) to add or join one thing to another thing

attached to: (*adj.*) fond of something or someone

attachment: (*n.*) something that is attached to something else

1 The girl was very ________________ her kitten and was very sad when it got lost.

2 Please reply to this email and ________________ a copy of your resume.

3 I'm sending three ________________ with this email.

C Answer the questions using your own words.

1 What was your most frustrating experience while shopping online?

____

2 What do you do to avoid getting spam in your emails?

____

3 What's the most encouraging advice you've received on social media?

____

4D

TED PLAYLIST

A group of schoolchildren use computers during a lesson.

IDEO's David Kelley says that product design has become much less about the hardware and more about the user experience. He's developing computer interfaces that adapt to human behavior and shows a video of this new, broader approach.

Linda Liukas is encouraging kids to see computers not as mechanical, boring, and complicated but as colorful, expressive machines they can play with. In this talk, she invites us to imagine a world where children will grow up to be optimistic about technology.

In this funny and enlightening talk, *New York Times* journalist David Pogue takes a close look at the unnecessarily complicated design of computer software. He highlights some of the worst mistakes developers make, and provides encouraging examples of products that get it right.

A Match the title of each TED Talk to the correct speaker.

1 Simplicity Sells ○ ○ **a** David Kelley

2 A Delightful Way to Teach Kids about Computers ○ ○ **b** Linda Liukas

3 Human-centered Design ○ ○ **c** David Pogue

B What is the theme of the playlist? Circle the best answer.

a how we interact with computers

b how to design computer software for children

c how computer software is improving

C Which speakers most likely said the following? Circle the correct answer.

1 "Unless we give them tools to build with computers, we are raising only consumers instead of creators."

a David Kelley **b** Linda Liukas **c** David Pogue

2 "Remember, the hard part is not deciding what features to add, it's deciding what to leave out."

a David Kelley **b** Linda Liukas **c** David Pogue

D Decide which talk you most want to watch. Watch it online at www.ted.com.

4E

WRITING Writing a review

A Read the sample review of an app.

Write one paragraph. Start by describing the website or product.

I downloaded an app to search for new movies. I really love sci-fi movies, so I want to be able to search for new sci-fi that are available online as soon as they come out. This app updates me with the latest movies and also tells me which ones are popular right now. It's more up-to-date than most of the other similar products on the market. The app downloads quickly and is easy to use. The main problem I had with this app was that there was no search box. It took me a long time to find the movies I liked.

Use some new words from this unit.

Then say why you liked this product and what its advantages are.

Describe one design flaw.

B Choose a website or an app that you have used. Answer the questions to plan your review.

1 What is the product for?

2 What did you like about it? What did you expect?

3 What are the advantages of it?

4 What were the design flaws?

C Now write your paragraph. Then complete the checklist below.

- ☐ Did you use correct spelling and punctuation?
- ☐ Did you use some new words from this unit?
- ☐ Did you compare different things?
- ☐ Did you explain how to improve the design?

5 Community Builders

5A

VOCABULARY Making communities better

Complete the sentences using the words in the box. One word is extra.

community	empowers	enhancing	entrepreneurs	facilities	underprivileged

1 She started a nonprofit organization for ________________ children to express themselves through art.

2 His success story inspired everyone in the ________________.

3 Education ________________ you. It gives you the tools you need to succeed in life.

4 The government spent a lot of money upgrading the ________________ in the library complex.

5 Steve Jobs, Mark Zuckerberg, and Bill Gates are all ________________ who started small but made it big.

LISTENING Creating green spaces

A ▶ 5.1 Listen. The two speakers are probably ___.

a politicians **b** neighbors **c** gardeners

B ▶ 5.1 Listen to the conversation again. Answer the questions.

1 What is focus of the project?

a building communities **b** developing urban gardens **c** eating more healthily

2 Where will this project be carried out?

a on building rooftops **b** people's backyards **c** at the library

3 Who can participate in this project?

a library members **b** local residents **c** friends

4 What are the advantages of this project? Check [✓] all that apply.

a You can grow your own vegetables. ☐

b There will be fewer empty buildings. ☐

c There will be more greenery in the city. ☐

d It will help reduce pollution. ☐

e It's a great way to make friends. ☐

f People can help and learn from one another. ☐

COMMUNICATION Talking about my community

A Complete the conversation. Number the sentences (**1–7**) in the correct order.

a ______ Really? Maybe you could suggest that your local council build one.

b ______ Well, it's quite peaceful and friendly.

c ______ I guess I could. Maybe if everyone at school supported the idea, they might consider it.

d __1__ Hi, I heard you recently moved to a new neighborhood. What's it like?

e ______ That's fantastic. I have to take a bus to the next town if I want to go to the library.

f ______ That's nice! Are there many facilities?

g ______ Yes, there's a supermarket and a library.

B Answer the questions using your own words.

1 What is your community like?

____

2 What kind of facilities do you have?

____

3 What would you improve in your community?

____

5B

LANGUAGE FOCUS Using the passive voice

A Rewrite each sentence using the passive form.

1 You can recycle rainwater from the roof.

Rainwater from the roof can be recycled.

2 They turned unused land into urban gardens.

Unused land ______________________________

3 Someone designed the cars to run on solar power.

The cars ______________________________

4 They converted a landfill into a skateboard park.

A landfill ______________________________

5 They built tunnels to divert traffic underground.

Tunnels ______________________________

B Complete the information with the passive form of the words provided.

The High Line, built in 1934, was an overhead railroad track in Manhattan, New York, which [1]__________ (use) to transport cargo into the city. However, when rail traffic started to decline, it was decided that the train tracks [2]__________ (need) any more and the city decided it should [3]__________ (tear down) and demolished. An organization called the Friends of the High Line [4]__________ (form) to fight against the demolition. A competition [5]__________ (hold) to find the best idea for the site. Ten years later, the High Line [6]__________ (redesign) as a beautiful urban park and garden. The old train tracks [7]__________ (convert) into a place where people can [8]__________ (surround) by green trees and flowers. Today, the High Line [9]__________ (visit) by hundreds of New Yorkers looking for some green space in the urban jungle. Further work on the project [10]__________ (plan), with ideas for museums, art spaces, and other facilities.

C Answer the questions.

1 What has changed recently in your city or neighborhood? __________

____

2 What kind of environmental improvements have been introduced? __________

____

3 What kinds of changes have been most beneficial to the city? __________

____

LISTENING FOCUS Word stress: *can* and *can't*

A ▶ **5.2** Listen to the sentences. Notice the difference in pronunciation between *can* and *can't*. *Can* is usually unstressed, and the vowel sound is reduced. *Can't* is usually stressed.

A bridge **can** be constructed.

The river **can** be cleaned.

The walls **can't** be painted.

The streets **can't** be repaired.

B ▶ **5.3** Listen. Circle the correct word to complete the sentences.

1 The water (**can** / **can't**) be used.

2 Trees (**can** / **can't**) be planted.

3 It (**can** / **can't**) be improved.

4 A sports center (**can** / **can't**) be built.

5 They (**can** / **can't**) be replaced.

C ▶ **5.4** Listen and write the sentences you hear.

1 __________

2 __________

3 __________

4 __________

5 __________

5C

READING

Read the passage and answer the questions.

1 Ruganzu Bruno Tusingwire is an eco-artist from Uganda. Orphaned as young child, he grew up in the countryside, surrounded by mountains and nature. Later, he moved to the capital city of Kampala and was shocked by the amount of waste all around him. There was so much waste it was becoming unmanageable. He realized it was important for everyone to work together as a community to reduce and recycle waste.

One of Tusingwire's projects was a playground made from recycled materials.

2 He started working on eco-art projects with some of his fellow students. They collected plastic bottles to make sculptures. They went to festivals and other public places and invited the public to help them finish the work by collecting more bottles. At first, people didn't understand what they were doing. But later, they joined in enthusiastically in creating art from waste.

3 Even though his projects were successful and popular, Tusingwire wanted to do more. He didn't only want to create art, he wanted to ensure that his project would create significant long-term benefits for his community. He wanted to help underprivileged children growing up in the slums, so he decided to create a playground for children. He talked with members of the community, including teachers, parents, and children. They all helped to collect bottles and other useable trash to make the playground, which they designed and built together.

4 The eco-art amusement park is a place where children can explore, climb, and play among the brightly colored climbing frames, life-sized board games, and swings—all made out of recycled tires, plastic bottles, and other trash. The children's smiles and shouts of laughter are proof of the success of the project.

5 Tusingwire's goal is to create many more similar amusement parks in other parts of Uganda. "Art is unifying," Tusingwire explains. "We can use what is around us to create treasure, employment opportunities, and make the environment better. There is a wonderful world of possibilities before us."

A What is the passage mainly about?

a A project to help raise money for underprivileged children in Uganda.

b The growing trash problem in Uganda's countryside.

c A young man who started a project to recycle waste and help a community.

B Circle the correct answer.

1 What inspired Tusingwire to start his eco-art projects?

a He saw how much trash there was in the countryside where he grew up.

b He helped clean up after a local festival and didn't know what to do with the trash.

c He was shocked by the amount of trash he saw when he moved to the city.

2 How was Tusingwire's eco-art playground different from his earlier projects?

a The playground was successful and popular.

b The playground was more than just a piece of art.

c The playgroud was built entirely from recycled waste.

3 What is Tusingwire's future goal?

a to teach others around the world about recycling

b to help people in his community get jobs

c to create similar parks around the country

LISTENING

A ▶ **5.5** Listen. What is the main purpose of the art exhibition?

a to persuade people to reduce trash

b to show different ways to recycle trash

c to empower people to create art

B ▶ **5.5** Listen again. Circle **T** for true or **F** for false.

1 The sculptures are made from trash.	**T**	**F**
2 The trash was collected from major cities.	**T**	**F**
3 Angela Pozzi built the sculptures by herself.	**T**	**F**
4 There are 143 billion kilograms of plastic in our oceans.	**T**	**F**
5 Trash in the oceans affects both animals and humans.	**T**	**F**

C Use the information (**a–i**) to complete the Venn diagram.

a It helps underprivileged people.

b It turns trash into art.

c It aims to raise awareness.

d It is an art exhibition held at a zoo.

e Trash was collected from beaches.

f Local communities were involved.

g It was started by an artist.

h It was done in the United States.

i It was done in Uganda.

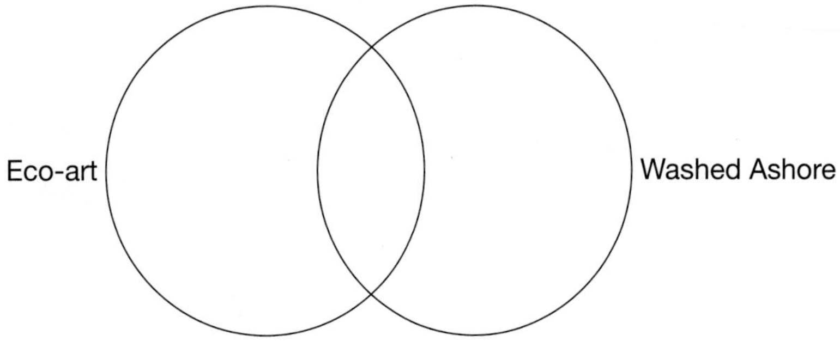

VOCABULARY BUILDING

A Complete the sentences using the words in the box.

dedication	ensure	proof	recruit	significant

1 There is scientific ____________ that the amount of trash in the ocean is growing.

2 Community group leaders usually ____________ volunteers to help with their projects.

3 Community projects need to ____________ that their work will continue after they have left.

4 The volunteers showed great ____________ to the recycling campaign.

5 Reducing and recycling trash can have a(n) ____________ impact on the environment.

B Some adjectives use the suffix *-ant*. Complete the sentences using the words in the box.

constant	distant	hesitant	vacant

1 The building was abandoned and had been ____________ for many years.

2 People were ____________ to join at first but now they're very enthusiastic.

3 We heard a ____________ crash from several kilometers away.

4 I couldn't sleep because of the ____________ noise from the airport.

5D

TED PLAYLIST

Vegetables are grown in the rooftop garden of a city building.

BUILDING A PARK IN THE SKY

New York City was planning to tear down the High Line, an old elevated railroad above the streets of Manhattan, when Robert Hammond and a few friends suggested: Why not make it a park? He talks about how he started a local community organization to save the High Line and make it into a park.

A PARK UNDERNEATH THE HUSTLE AND BUSTLE OF NEW YORK CITY

Dan Barasch and James Ramsey have a crazy plan—to create the Lowline, an underground park the size of a football field underneath New York City. The two are building it in an abandoned trolley bus station, which was last used in 1948. They're using technology to bring sunlight from above-ground to down below.

A GUERILLA GARDENER IN SOUTH CENTRAL LA

Ron Finley plants vegetable gardens in South Central Los Angeles—on abandoned land at the edges of the street. Why? For fun, for beauty, and to offer some alternative to fast food. His long term goal is to make his community a more peaceful and beautiful place to live.

A Match each speaker to the topic of their TED Talk.

1 Robert Hammond ○ ○ **a** growing food on city streets
2 Dan Barasch ○ ○ **b** creating a park underground
3 Ron Finley ○ ○ **c** transforming a railroad

B Which speakers most likely said the following? Circle the correct answer.

1 "I first read about it in the *New York Times*, in an article that said it was going to be demolished."
a Dan Barasch **b** Robert Hammond **c** Ron Finley

2 "A lot of people said to us, 'Oh, it kind of looks like the High Line underground.'"
a Dan Barasch **b** Robert Hammond **c** Ron Finley

3 "I planted a food forest in front of my house."
a Dan Barasch **b** Robert Hammond **c** Ron Finley

C What do all three speakers have in common?

a they created a kind of park **b** they teach new skills to others **c** they used unwanted spaces

D Decide which talk you most want to watch. Watch it online at www.ted.com.

5E

WRITING Making a suggestion

A Read the sample letter to a local city council requesting for a community garden in the neighborhood.

Write two paragraphs. In the first paragraph, describe why you are suggesting this idea.

In the second paragraph, describe the benefits of this project.

Dear Sir/Madam,

I'm writing to suggest the creation of a community garden in my neighborhood. There are many people who live in apartments who don't have gardens but would love to grow their own vegetables. There is also a lot of abandoned land that is not being used. I think that many people would welcome the opportunity to use this land to grow their own food.

The benefits of this would be that the abandoned land is used for a good purpose, community members would get to grow and eat healthy food, and it would improve their sense of community when they work together. In my opinion, it would make our community a happier and healthier place.

Yours sincerely,

Scott

Use some new words from this unit.

Use phrases like "I suggest," "I think," and "In my opinion."

B Write a letter to your city council requesting a new playground for children. Answer the questions to plan your letter.

1 Describe the project.

2 Why is it needed?

3 What are the benefits?

4 How will your neighborhood change?

C Now write your letter. Then complete the checklist below.

- ☐ Did you use correct spelling and punctuation?
- ☐ Did you use some new words from this unit?
- ☐ Did you use passive forms?
- ☐ Did you explain how your project will improve the community?

6 Clear Communication

6A

VOCABULARY Using communication collocations

A Complete the paragraph using the words in the box.

have	having	make	making	post	write	writing

Whether you're [1] __________ a conversation, [2] __________ a speech, or [3] __________ an email, it is important to adapt your communication style to the medium you are using. When you [4] __________ a meeting, your communication style will usually be more formal than when you [5] __________ a phone call. Similarly, when you [6] __________ an update on social media, it will usually be simpler and more direct than when you [7] __________ a letter.

B Correct the mistake in each sentence.

1. Have you had to give a phone call in English?
2. How often do you make letters to your friends?
3. Do you prefer giving text messages or emails?
4. When was the last time you posted a speech in public?
5. Do you sometimes make photos online?

LISTENING Communication styles

A ▶ 6.1 Listen to an expert giving advice to managers about communication. What are the three tips the expert gives? Complete the sentences.

1. Use different __________ channels.
2. Use a __________ that creates a supportive atmosphere.
3. Show that you appreciate your team's __________.

B ▶ 6.1 Listen again. Would the speaker agree with the following statements? Circle **Y** for yes or **N** for no.

1 It's okay for managers to hold group meetings.	**Y**	**N**
2 One-to-one meetings are a waste of time.	**Y**	**N**
3 Managers should use a commanding tone.	**Y**	**N**
4 A manager should thank staff for their time after meetings.	**Y**	**N**

COMMUNICATION Talking about communication preferences

A Complete the conversations using the phrases in the box.

I saw it on YouTube.	**I posted them on Facebook.**
I'll send it in an email.	**You can buy them online.**

1 A: Have you checked out our school's new website?
B: No, can you send me the link?
A: Sure. ______________________________

2 A: Did you see my photos?
B: Which photos? Did you send them by email?
A: No, ______________________________

3 A: Did you get tickets for the concert?
B: Not yet. Where do I get them?
A: ______________________________

4 A: Look at this video. It shows you how to play the guitar!
B: Cool! Where did you find it?
A: ______________________________

B Complete the conversation. Circle the correct words.

A: Hey, Martin, [1] (**check** / **share**) this out!
B: Hi, Lisa. What's up?
A: My friend [2] (**checked** / **posted**) a video of his band on YouTube. Want to see?
B: Sure. Wow, they sound great! Can you send me the [3] (**post** / **link**)?
A: Of course. If you really like it, could you [4] (**share** / **post**) a comment? They'll really appreciate it.
B: No problem, I'll [5] (**share** / **check**) the link with my friends too.

6B

LANGUAGE FOCUS Describing types of communicators

A Complete the conversation. Circle the correct words.

A: Have you told the boss you want [1] (**to quit** / **quitting**) yet?
B: Not yet. I'm planning [2] (**to send** / **sending**) him an email today.
A: An email? I'd strongly recommend [3] (**to talk** / **talking**) to him face to face.
B: But I'm worried that he'll try to persuade me [4] (**to stay** / **staying**). An email seems much easier.
A: Well, it's your decision, but I know he'll dislike [5] (**to hear** / **hearing**) this kind of news via email.

B Rewrite each sentence so that it has the same meaning. Use the words provided.

1 I don't usually write long emails. (avoid)

____

2 I think you should create your own blog. (recommend)

____

3 Video chatting is a good way to stay in touch with friends who live far away. (help)

____

4 A smartphone means you can stay in touch wherever you are. (allow)

____

C Complete the sentences using your own words.

1 I usually ______________ my friends every day.
2 I like ______________ my family because ______________.
3 ______________ allows me to ______________ with my co-workers.
4 I avoid ______________ because ______________.
5 ______________ helps me ______________.

LISTENING FOCUS Intonation when agreeing and disagreeing

A **6.2** We usually use rising intonation when we disagree with someone. We often use falling intonation when we agree. Listen and repeat what you hear.

A: I really don't like group meetings. **B:** Really? I find them really useful.
A: I really don't like group meetings. **B:** Yeah. They can be really boring.

B **6.3** Listen to the sentences. Draw arrows to show rising or falling intonation in B's replies. Listen and check your answers.

1 **A:** Email is so old-fashioned. **B:** Yeah. I never use it these days.
2 **A:** I really don't like using Facebook. **B:** Really? I use it every day.
3 **A:** I hate speaking in public. **B:** Yeah? I actually quite enjoy it.

C **6.4** Listen to the intonation in the sentences below. Do you think the person is agreeing or disagreeing with someone? Circle **A** for agreeing or **D** for disagreeing.

1 I thought it was really interesting. **A** **D**
2 I thought it was too short. **A** **D**
3 I found the end part the most interesting. **A** **D**
4 Her delivery was really good. **A** **D**

D **6.5** Listen to the full conversation and check your answers in **C**.

6C

READING

Read the passage and answer the questions below.

1 Maddalena Bearzi is a marine biologist. She believes there are many things that scientists can do to help the general public understand difficult scientific concepts. She has four simple suggestions to help scientists make science more accessible to the rest of us.

2 Firstly, scientists need to find ways of explaining complex things in everyday terms. They should learn from some of the great scientific communicators, such as Albert Einstein or Carl Sagan, and relate information to everyday situations so their audience can better grasp any complex concepts.

Maddalena Bearzi believes scientists need to communicate better with the general public.

3 A scientist should also assume that their readers or viewers are as smart and curious as they are. The average person just doesn't know what a scientist knows. There is no doubt that scientists and the public often have different communication styles. So scientists need to know how to talk to their audience without boring them with scientific talk!

4 Science writers can learn a lot from fiction writers. They should share their adventures in the lab using engaging and inspiring plots, odd characters, or mysteries. True stories can easily be written to sound more like "fiction" to gain popular appeal. If scientists can talk about their personal feelings and experiences, it will make their stories come alive.

5 Finally, scientists should avoid using graphs and tables if they can, and, where possible, not use text on their presentation slides. Audiences should be engaged with exciting images or even cartoon strips to lighten up a talk.

6 The goal of a scientist, as either writer or speaker, is to be accessible to everyone regardless of their background. Now, more than ever, it is important to recognize these gaps by writing or speaking in a way that bridges them.

A Match the headings to the correct paragraphs.

1 Paragraph 2 ○	○ **a** Use pictures if you can.
2 Paragraph 3 ○	○ **b** Use simple and easy-to-understand language.
3 Paragraph 4 ○	○ **c** Tell interesting stories.
4 Paragraph 5 ○	○ **d** Don't underestimate your audience.

B Would Maddelena Bearzi agree with the following statements? Circle **Y** for yes or **N** for no.

1 Albert Einstein was good at communicating with the public.	**Y**	**N**
2 Scientists should realize most people are not as smart as they are.	**Y**	**N**
3 Most scientists communicate in a different style to the general public.	**Y**	**N**
4 Scientific ideas can be communicated effectively through stories.	**Y**	**N**
5 Scientists should use graphs whenever they can.	**Y**	**N**

LISTENING

A ▶ **6.6** Listen. Which sentence best describes the book?

a It is a detailed description of plants and animals.

b It combines personal stories with scientific descriptions.

c It is a handbook for how to teach science.

B ▶ **6.6** Listen again. Circle **T** for true, **F** for false, or **NG** for not given.

1 The speaker found the book interesting.	**T**	**F**	**NG**
2 The author engages her readers by asking them questions.	**T**	**F**	**NG**
3 In the book, the author talks about her childhood.	**T**	**F**	**NG**
4 The book contains photos taken by the author.	**T**	**F**	**NG**
5 The author says her work as a scientist was always exciting.	**T**	**F**	**NG**

C **CRITICAL THINKING** Do you think the author has followed the guidelines given in the reading passage? Give examples to support your answer.

____

____

____

VOCABULARY BUILDING

A Complete the sentences using the words in the box.

analogy	concise	last	span	technical

1 The article included a very long and detailed explanation. It wasn't a very ________________ description.

2 His argument was too difficult to understand. He used a lot of scientific and ________________ words.

3 The first study only lasted two years, but the second one had a time ________________ of ten years.

4 My teacher compared sound waves to waves in the ocean, which was a useful ________________.

5 When carrying out community projects, it's important that the changes will ________________.

B Complete the sentences using the words in **bold**.

attention span: the amount of time you can concentrate
life span: the length of your life
time span: a length or period of time

1 The average two-year-old has a(n) ________________ of about five minutes.

2 Elephants have a(n) ________________ of up to 70 years.

3 Future research may focus on specific areas over a shorter ________________.

C Answer the questions using your own words.

1 What kind of analogy could a scientist use to explain the size of the solar system?

____

2 Do you have a short or long attention span? Why do you say so?

____

3 What is the average life span of the people in your country?

____

A speaker shows a slide at the Warsaw Medical Congress for Young Scientists.

TEDTALKS

6D

TED PLAYLIST

The Large Hadron Collider (LHC) at CERN

CERN'S SUPERCOLLIDER

Physicist Brian Cox has two jobs: working with the Large Hadron Collider at CERN, and explaining science to the general public. In this talk, Cox brings us along on a tour of this massive project, and explains the LHC's search for new particles in an engaging, accessible way.

THE MOST MYSTERIOUS STAR IN THE UNIVERSE

Something massive, with roughly 1,000 times the area of Earth, is blocking the light coming from a distant star known as KIC 8462852, and nobody is quite sure what it is. In this talk, Tabetha Boyajian gives us a look at how scientists search for and test hypotheses when faced with the unknown.

HOW WE'LL FIND LIFE ON OTHER PLANETS

Astronomer Aomawa Shields searches for clues that life might exist elsewhere in the universe by examining the atmospheres of distant exoplanets. When she isn't exploring the heavens, the classically trained actor looks for ways to engage young women in the sciences using theater, writing, and visual art.

A What is the theme of this playlist?

a discoveries in science **b** exploring the solar system **c** combining science and art

B Check [✓] the correct column(s).

Which speaker(s)...	Brian Cox	Tabetha Boyajian	Aomawa Shields
1 is interested in a mysterious star?			
2 tries to help women scientists?			
3 talks about a very big science project?			
4 asks questions about life on other planets?			
5 educates the public during their free time?			

C Decide which talk you most want to watch. Watch it online at www.ted.com.

6E

WRITING Giving an explanation

A Read the sample answer about a description of a game.

My favorite board game is Scrabble. Imagine creating a giant crossword: players build this "crossword" by adding one word to it at a time.

Scrabble can be played by two to four people. You need a set of small wooden or plastic squares—each one has a letter printed on it. Different letters have different values; for example, A is worth one point, and Q is worth 10 points. Each player gets seven letter squares. You use a board that is marked with squares. The board has colored squares that can double or triple the points of a letter, or word, placed on that square.

Remember to explain any steps carefully and to emphasize key points.

The aim of the game is to form words by placing your letters on the board to gain points for each one. The winner is the person with the most points at the end of the game.

Make your main message short and clear.

B Describe a game or sport that you like. Answer the questions to plan your description.

1 What is the name of the game?

2 What are the rules of the game?

3 Is there an analogy you can use to explain the game?

4 How do you win the game?

C Now write your description. Then complete the checklist below.

- ☐ Did you use correct spelling and punctuation?
- ☐ Did you use some new words from this unit?
- ☐ Did you explain the rules of the game or sport?
- ☐ Did you use analogies to describe your game or sport?

7 Identity

7A

VOCABULARY Describing identity

A Complete the sentences using the words in the box.

background	**factor**	**have a lot in common**	**migrant**
multicultural	**sense of identity**	**traditional**	

1 A ______________________ city has people of different groups from different places.

2 A ______________________ is something that affects an event, decision, or situation.

3 ______________________ customs, beliefs, or methods have existed for a long time without changing.

4 If you ______________________ with someone, you share the same interests, attitudes, or opinions.

5 A ______________________ is someone who moves from one country to another, often to find work.

6 Your ______________________ is how you feel about yourself.

7 A person's ______________________ refers to their social class, education, training, and experience.

B Complete the paragraph using the correct form of the words in **A**.

My [1] ______________________ is strongly influenced by the place where I grew up. I was born in London, a [2] ______________________ city that people from many different cultures call home. Different ethnic groups retain many aspects of their [3] ______________________ culture while at the same time mixing with people from different [4] ______________________. I believe we all [5] ______________________ and it's good for cultures to influence and learn from each other.

LISTENING Multicultural experiences

A ▶ **7.1** Listen to the talk. Circle the best answer.

1 The talk is about migrants from ___.

a North Africa **b** Eastern Europe **c** the West Indies

2 Why did the migrants leave their home country?

a to find work **b** to escape war **c** because of a natural disaster

3 Why did the British government "open its doors" to the migrants?

a They wanted to make London more multicultural.

b They needed people to help fight in the Second World War.

c They needed workers to help rebuild after the Second World War.

B Answer the questions in your own words.

1 What do you think the migrants liked about living in Britain?

___

2 What do you think the migrants disliked about living in Britain?

___

COMMUNICATION: Talking about your background

A Complete the conversation. Number the sentences (**1–8**) in the correct order.

a ___ Well, it's been almost ten years since I came to Brazil.

b _1_ Hi! Nice to meet you. Where are you from?

c ___ I've heard Tokyo's a beautiful place. So, have you been living here long?

d ___ That's good. Do you go back often?

e ___ Well, I try to visit my family at least once a year.

f ___ Wow! That's a long time. Do you miss home?

g ___ Hello, nice to meet you too. I'm from Tokyo.

h ___ Yeah, I did at first. But I got used to it after that.

B Answer the questions using your own words.

1 Where does your family originally come from?

___

2 How much does your family history affect your sense of identity?

___

7B

LANGUAGE FOCUS Discussing current events

A Circle the correct words to complete the conversation.

A: So, how are you finding life here?

B: Oh, it's great. But I still haven't [1] (**found** / **been finding**) a job yet.

A: How long have you [2] (**looked** / **been looking**) for one?

B: A couple of months now. I think I've [3] (**sent** / **been sending**) 10 applications this week alone.

A: Have you [4] (**had** / **been having**) any replies?

B: Not many. But I have an interview tomorrow. I've [5] (**read** / **been reading**) up on the company all day!

B Write a question for each response using your own words.

1 **A:** How long ______________________________ here?

B: About two years.

2 **A:** What ______________________________?

B: I was a waiter for one year, but now I'm a coffee house manager.

3 **A:** ______________________________ at college, too?

B: Yes, I'm studying English literature.

4 **A:** ______________________________?

B: No, it's impossible to save money—everything is so expensive here!

C Unscramble the questions. Then answer them using your own words.

1 What / have / been / recently / up to / you

Q: ______________________________?

A: ______________________________.

2 Have / overseas / been / lately / you

Q: ______________________________?

A: ______________________________.

3 long / been / English / How / have / you / studying

Q: ______________________________?

A: ______________________________.

LISTENING FOCUS Unstressed words

A ▶ **7.2** When *have* is used as an auxiliary verb, it is often unstressed and the vowel sound is reduced. Listen and repeat what you hear.

What have you been doing?

How long have you been living here?

Where has she been staying?

B ▶ **7.3** Listen. Circle the sentence you hear.

1 **a** How long will you be traveling? **b** How long have you been traveling?

2 **a** What will you be studying? **b** What have you been studying?

3 **a** Where will you be working? **b** Where have you been working?

4 **a** Why will you be coming home late? **b** Why have you been coming home late?

C ▶ **7.4** Listen and write the sentences you hear.

1 ______________________________

2 ______________________________

3 ______________________________

4 ______________________________

7C

READING

Read the passage and answer the questions.

1 New York City—also known as "the melting pot"—is one of the most multicultural cities in the world. Here are some of the neighborhoods you may want to visit when you're there.

A lion dance takes place in Chinatown, New York, as part of Chinese New Year celebrations.

2 New York's Chinatown is one of the biggest Chinese neighborhoods in the country. Chinese immigrants first started coming to the United States in the 1850s. They came to find gold during the California Gold Rush, and to build the great railroads. However, they later moved east to find work in the wool factories, and in the cigar, shoe, and clothing industries. Today's Chinatown is a busy, lively district where you can find fresh fruit and vegetable stalls, open-air fish markets, and parks where you can see people practicing *tai chi* or playing Chinese chess.

3 The bustling vibrant neighborhood known as Little Odessa is located in Brooklyn's Brighton Beach. Russians started to immigrate to New York back in the 1800s, escaping famine and disease in their homeland. This neighborhood is full of traditional Russian tea shops, delis, and restaurants. You'll hear Russian spoken in many of the stores. The Millennium Theater features shows by Russian theater groups, musicians, and dancers.

4 Richmond Hill is home to a large community from Guyana. Immigration from Guyana increased in the 1960s and 1970s due to economic hardships and the need for skilled workers in the United States. Here in Little Guyana, you can see women in colorful saris, hear the sound of *chutney* (a mix of reggae and Indian music), and enjoy street food such as *roti* pancakes filled with curried chickpeas, Caribbean spices, and coconut.

A What is main purpose of the passage? Circle the best answer.

- **a** to show the difficulties faced by many immigrants living in New York
- **b** to give a brief history of immigration in New York
- **c** to give examples of places that show how multicultural New York is

B Circle the best answers according to the information in the passage.

1 According to the passage, what does the term "melting pot" mean?

- **a** an area where people of different races live
- **b** a market where you can buy food from different countries

2 Which community was the earliest to arrive in New York?

a the Chinese **b** the Russians **c** the Guyanians

3 Why did the Chinese immigrants come to New York?

- **a** there were terrible diseases in their country
- **b** there were jobs available for them

4 Why did the Russians come to New York?

- **a** there wasn't enough jobs for everyone in their country
- **b** there was a shortage of food in their country

LISTENING

A ▶ 7.5 Listen. What is the talk mainly about?

- **a** different ways to define multiculturalism
- **b** problems with multicultural societies
- **c** how multicultural societies have developed all over the world

B ▶ 7.5 Listen again. Circle the best answer.

1 Why is Chad mentioned in the talk?

- **a** It is a country with many official languages.
- **b** It is an example of an ethnically diverse country.

2 What do Singapore and India have in common?

- **a** In both countries, English is an official language.
- **b** Both countries have four official languages.

3 Which statement would the speaker most likely agree with?

- **a** It's very difficult to define multiculturalism.
- **b** Multiculturalism is best defined in terms of ethinic diversity.

C **CRITICAL THINKING** "People don't always fit into cultural categories." Do you agree or disagree with this statement? Give reasons for your answer.

____

____

VOCABULARY BUILDING

A Complete the sentences using the word in the box.

conflicts	**diverse**	**era**	**influx**	**undertaking**	**vibrant**

1 There is a(n) ______________ of tourists every year in the summer months.

2 The increase in migration is due to a lot of ______________ factors.

3 Moving to another country with your family is a serious ______________.

4 Little India is a busy and ______________ neighborhood in Singapore.

5 We live in a(n) ______________ of information and communication.

6 There can sometimes be misunderstandings between people of different ethnic backgrounds that result in ______________.

B Write the noun forms of the words in the correct column.

Examples: vibrant – vibrancy, tolerant – tolerance

dominant	**important**	**infant**	**pregnant**	**reluctant**	**tolerant**	**vacant**	**vibrant**

-ancy	-ance

C Complete the sentences using the words in the box.

dominant	**infant**	**reluctant**	**tolerant**	**vacant**

1 Society is becoming more ______________ of difference. People from different ethnic backgrounds can be found in almost all cities around the world.

2 As they got on the plane, the mother held her ______________ son close to her.

3 The house next to hers had been ______________ for so long, so she was surprised to find someone had moved in during the night.

4 She was a ______________ figure in the country's political scene.

5 He knew it was wrong, so he was ______________ to accept the bribe being offered to him.

7D

TED PLAYLIST

Chimamanda Adichie on stage at TED

DON'T ASK WHERE I'M FROM, ASK WHERE I'M A LOCAL

When someone asks you where you're from, do you sometimes not know how to answer? Writer Taiye Selasi speaks on behalf of "multilocal" people, who feel at home in the town where they grew up, the city they live now, and maybe another place or two. "How can I come from a country?" she asks. "How can a human being come from a concept?"

EMBRACING OTHERNESS, EMBRACING MYSELF

Actor Thandie Newton tells the story of finding her "otherness"—first, as a child growing up in two distinct cultures, and then as an actor playing with many different selves. Growing up in England, she knew that she didn't fit in, and felt that she lacked a sense of identity. Later, she found ways to use this experience in her acting career.

THE DANGER OF A SINGLE STORY

Our lives, our cultures, are composed of many overlapping stories. Novelist Chimamanda Adichie tells the story of how she found her authentic cultural voice—and warns that if we hear only a single story about another person or country, we risk stereotyping them.

A What is the theme of the playlist? Circle the best answer.

a What is my identity? **b** What is my country? **c** Why am I here?

B Which speaker most likely said the following? Circle the correct answer.

1 "The single story creates stereotypes, and the problem with stereotypes is not that they are untrue, but that they are incomplete."

a Taiye Selasi **b** Chimamanda Adichie **c** Thandie Newton

2 "To me, a country—this thing that could be born, die, expand, contract—hardly seemed the basis for understanding a human being."

a Taiye Selasi **b** Chimamanda Adichie **c** Thandie Newton

3 "My panic at not having a self that fit, and the confusion that came from my self being rejected, created anxiety, shame, and hopelessness, which kind of defined me for a long time."

a Taiye Selasi **b** Chimamanda Adichie **c** Thandie Newton

C Decide which talk you most want to watch. Watch it online at www.ted.com.

7E

WRITING A reflection

A Read the sample passage about factors that are important to a person's identity.

In the first paragraph, say the factors that influence your sense of identity.

I think two of the most important factors influencing my sense of identity is where I was born and the place I grew up. I was born and grew up in Vancouver, Canada. I think people here are quite relaxed and enjoy their lives. Their free time and friends are more important than work or career. And that's pretty much how I am as well.

Use some new words from this unit.

An important influence in my character has been my parents. Both my parents were <u>migrants</u> from China and they had quite a traditional approach to my education. They always encouraged me to study hard and to be ambitious. I have a career as a doctor and I think that's shaped my personal identity, too. I see myself as someone who wants to help others and prevent suffering.

In the second paragraph, say the factors that influence your character.

B What factors define your sense of identity? Answer the questions to plan your passage.

1 Who or what influences your sense of identity?

2 How do these influences shape your identity?

3 What factors influence your character?

C Now write your passage. Then complete the checklist below.

- ☐ Did you use correct spelling and punctuation?
- ☐ Did you use some new words from this unit?
- ☐ Did you mention the factors that shape your identity?
- ☐ Did you describe how they shaped your identity?

8 Transportation Solutions

8A

VOCABULARY Describing modes of transportation

A Complete the sentences. Circle the correct words.

1 Are you going to take a _______ home?

a taxi **b** car **c** bicycle

2 Does your uncle drive a _______?

a bus **b** motorbike **c** bicycle

3 How often do you ride a _______ to work?

a plane **b** car **c** bicycle

4 Do you usually take a _______ to your office?

a bicycle **b** car **c** bus

5 Look! There's Joanna. She's just getting off the _______.

a bus **b** taxi **c** car

B Answer the questions using your own words.

How often do you ...

1 ride a bicycle? ____.

2 take a taxi? ____.

LISTENING An unusual commute

A ▶ **8.1** Listen. Circle the best answer.

1 The main purpose of the bike-sharing programs is to ___.

a encourage people to exercise **b** reduce the number of vehicles on the road **c** reduce the cost of commuting

2 Which of these is true about the bike-sharing scheme?

a You must return your bike to the same place you borrowed it from.

b One bike can be used by many users in the same day.

B Complete the table with information from the talk.

	London	Paris	Hangzhou
Number of bikes	11,000		
Number of bike stations			2,400
Annual cost		€29	not given

COMMUNICATION Talking about your daily routine

A Choose the best response to each question.

1. How do you get to work?
   a I usually take the bus. **b** It takes a long time.
2. How long does it take for you to get to the office?
   a I'm always late. **b** More than an hour!
3. You have a short commute, don't you?
   a Yeah, it only takes 15 minutes. **b** No, I prefer to drive.
4. Have you ever thought about cycling to work?
   a No, it's too far. **b** Yes, good idea.

B Write questions to complete the conversation.

A: ____?

B: I usually take the bus.

A: ____?

B: Well, my commute takes about 40 minutes, from my house to the office.

A: ____?

B: I did try it once, but it's too dangerous to ride a bike on that route.

A: ____?

B: I could do, but the subway station's quite far from my house.

8B

LANGUAGE FOCUS Making travel predictions

A Circle the option that is closest in meaning to each statement.

1. It is going to be sunny all weekend.
   a It won't rain all weekend. **b** It might rain all weekend.
2. There isn't going to be a band at the party.
   a There might not be a band at the party. **b** There won't be a band at the party.
3. The river's going to flood if the rain doesn't stop.
   a If it keeps raining, the river will flood. **b** If it keeps raining, the river might flood.

B ▶ **8.2** Listen. Do the ideas below match what you hear? Circle **Y** for yes or **N** for no.

1 Most cars will use electricity instead of gas in the future.	**Y**	**N**
2 There will be high-speed long-distance trains underground.	**Y**	**N**
3 Soon, space travel is going to be affordable for many people.	**Y**	**N**
4 Air pollution might get better in the future.	**Y**	**N**

C Complete the predictions about the future using your own words.

1 Most people ______________________________. (driverless cars)

2 Driving on highways ______________________________. (safe)

3 Highways ______________________________. (crowded)

4 People ______________________________. (learn to drive)

5 It ______________________________. (own a car)

6 There ______________________________. (pollution and noise)

LISTENING FOCUS Contraction of *will*

A ▶ **8.3** The verb *will* is usually contracted in spoken English. Listen and repeat what you hear.

Contractions with personal pronouns are used in informal writing.

I'll go to the moon for a holiday.

They'll invent a way to live longer.

I'll be able to travel in time.

Contractions with nouns are used only when speaking.

Robots'll replace humans in the workplace.

Cars'll get faster and safer.

Cities'll get bigger and bigger.

B ▶ **8.4** Listen. Circle the option you hear.

1 We (**travel** / **'ll travel**) by car to work.

2 Neighborhoods (**will become** / **become**) more crowded.

3 We (**communicate** / **'ll communicate**) via video chat.

4 Most people (**live** / **will live**) in large cities.

5 Robots (**do** / **will do**) a variety of jobs.

6 I (**work** / **'ll work**) remotely from home.

C ▶ **8.5** Listen to each question. Circle the best response.

1 a Yes, I think they will. **b** Yes, I think they do.

2 a No, they won't. **b** No, I don't think they do.

3 a Yes, they will. **b** Yes, I think they do.

8C

READING

Read the passage and answer the questions.

1 As cities have grown in size and population, scientists have come up with ways to improve public transportation systems. Here are some of the ideas that might soon be seen in our cities.

A model demonstrating the concept of the straddling bus

Car trains

2 Developed in Europe, the SARTRE (Safe Road Trains for the Environment) project is an interesting alternative to driving. Cars going in the same direction are grouped together so they travel as a single unit. Each car in this system is equipped with high-tech cameras, radars, and laser sensors so that they are linked together wirelessly. The lead car is operated by a professional driver, and the other cars travel on autopilot behind it. The benefits: the cars drive more safely, there's less congestion, and fuel consumption is lower. Plus, drivers in the cars behind can relax and read a book or watch a movie on their way to work!

The straddling bus

3 In China, engineers have come up with a creative public transport solution—giant buses that drive over cars. The buses run on very thin tracks between car lanes. Each bus can carry up to 1,200 people. They are cheaper than building a subway system, and since they are powered by solar power and electricity, they may help to reduce pollution too.

Cable cars

4 Cable cars are already common in countries such as Switzerland and Bolivia. Recently, there have been plans to use them as a way of solving major traffic congestion in large cities. Mexico City is considering a cable car system that runs horizontally above traffic. Traveling at a speed of 15 kilometers per hour, they would be much faster than the road traffic, which moves at an average speed of 8 kilometers per hour.

A Match each piece of technology to its main purpose.

1 Cable cars	o	o	**a** to make travelling by car safer and more fuel efficient
2 The straddling bus	o	o	**b** to transport large numbers of commuters at one time
3 Car trains	o	o	**c** to provide an alternative to using roads

B Circle **T** for true, **F** for false, or **NG** for not given.

1 The car train carries passengers above the traffic.	**T**	**F**	**NG**
2 The car train passengers will use their own cars.	**T**	**F**	**NG**
3 The straddling bus is environmentally friendly.	**T**	**F**	**NG**
4 The straddling bus will be operated by a computer.	**T**	**F**	**NG**
5 The cable car system will move more slowly than road traffic.	**T**	**F**	**NG**

LISTENING

A ▶ **8.6** Listen. Which sentence best summarizes the talk?

a Traffic congestion is increasing in all growing cities.

b There are many ways to reduce traffic congestion.

c We need to reduce the number of cars in cities.

B ▶ **8.6** Listen again. Circle the correct answer.

1 A congestion charge is ___.

a a special fee to travel by car on weekends

b a special fee to travel by public transport

c a special fee to drive in the city on weekdays

2 HOV lanes are ___.

a highway lanes that are usually congested

b special lanes for cars with more than one person in them

c special lanes for drivers with no passengers

3 What is one disadvantage of the electronically-linked vehicle concept?

a All vehicles must be electronically linked.

b It requires large numbers of vehicles going to the same destination.

c There is a high possibility of vehicles crashing into one another.

C **CRITICAL THINKING.** Which idea from the passage or talk do you think is the best way to solve traffic congestion in cities? Give reasons for your answer.

____

____

____

VOCABULARY BUILDING

A Complete the sentences using the correct form of the words in the box.

battery	carry	different	sure	walk

1 A **portable** computer is one that is small enough to be ______________ around.

2 An **alternative** form of transport is ______________ from existing ones.

3 Electric cars need a station where they can **charge** their ______________.

4 **Pedestrians** are people who ______________ along a street.

5 If a plan is **guaranteed** to work, then you are ______________ of its success.

B Choose a word from the box to replace each word in **bold**.

charged in court	charged a fee	charged

1 We were terrified when the bear **ran** at us. ______________

2 He was **sentenced by a judge** for stealing from his company. ______________

3 If you want to use the public bicycles, you will be **asked to pay money**. ______________

C Answer the questions using your own words.

1 Do you have any portable devices? What are they?

____

____

2 If your preferred mode of transportation is not available, what alternatives do you use?

____

____

3 How often do you need to charge your cell phone?

____

____

8D

TED PLAYLIST

A prototype of a futuristic electric car

EXCUSE ME, MAY I RENT YOUR CAR?

A decade ago, Robin Chase founded Zipcar in the U.S., now the largest car-sharing company in the world. Now she's exploring the next level of car-sharing: Buzzcar, a French start-up that lets people rent their own cars to others. How does it work and how is it changing our view of car ownership?

UBER'S PLAN TO GET MORE PEOPLE IN FEWER CARS

As the company took off, co-founder Travis Kalanick wondered if there was a way to get people using Uber along the same routes to share rides, reducing costs and pollution at the same time. The result: uberPOOL, the company's carpooling service, which in its first eight months took 13 million kilometers off the roads and 1,400 tons of carbon dioxide out of the air in Los Angeles.

NEW YORK'S STREETS? NOT SO MEAN ANY MORE

In this funny and thought-provoking talk, Janette Sadik-Khan, transportation commissioner of New York City, shares projects that have reshaped traffic, including pedestrian zones in Times Square, high-performance buses, and a 6,000-cycle-strong bike share. Her principle: "Do bold experiments that are cheap to try out."

A What is the theme of this playlist?

a reducing car pollution **b** innovations in transportation **c** how to make travel faster

B Answer the questions.

1 Which speakers founded a company?

a Robin Chase and Janette Sadik-Khan **b** Robin Chase and Travis Kalanick **c** Kalanick and Janette Sadik-Khan

2 Which speaker focuses on public transportation?

a Robin Chase **b** Travis Kalanick **c** Janette Sadik-Khan

3 Which speaker adapted an existing service to make it better?

a Robin Chase **b** Travis Kalanick **c** Janette Sadik-Khan

C Decide which talk you most want to watch. Watch it online at www.ted.com.

8E

WRITING Describing an invention

A Read the sample passage about a new personal transportation device.

Start by saying who your transportation device is for.

The personal transportation device we've created is for people who commute by bus or train but might have difficulty with walking long distances to their bus stops.

The device can be folded up into your backpack. It stores energy in a solar battery. It's made from light plastic that is flexible and very strong. When you want to use it, you simply unfold it and stand it on the ground. It looks just like a chair with roller wheels. As soon as you sit on it, it will start to move forward. When you reach your destination, leave it out in the sun to recharge.

In the second paragraph, describe the device and how it works.

In the third paragraph, explain the benefits.

The advantages of this device are that you can use it when you need to go short distances between different modes of transport and then put it in your backpack again when you get on a train or bus.

B Think about a new transportation device that will be useful in your city. Answer the questions to plan your passage.

1 Who is your transportation device for?

2 What does it look like?

3 How does it work?

4 What are the benefits?

C Now write your passage. Then complete the checklist below.

- ☐ Did you use correct spelling and punctuation?
- ☐ Did you use some new words from this unit?
- ☐ Did you explain how your device works?
- ☐ Did you explain the benefits of your device?

9 New Words

9A

VOCABULARY Describing language

A Complete the information using the words in the box.

degrade	standard	usage

1 The word *blog* was only invented in 1999, but it is now considered ________________ English.

2 Some people fear that the acceptance of slang words will cause the language to ________________.

3 Dictionary editors study data on the ________________ and popularity of new words.

B Circle the correct answer.

1 When would someone be most likely to use **slang**?

a during a presentation **b** during a phone call with a close friend

2 Which of these is an **accepted** way of speaking during an interview?

a Hi, I'm Susan. I'm here for an interview.

b Heya dude! I'm here for a chat with the boss!

LISTENING Collecting words

A ▶ 9.1 Listen. What is the talk mainly about?

a the life of Samuel Johnson

b new words that have recently been added to dictionaries

c how dictionaries today are different from those in the past

B ▶ 9.1 Listen again. Check [✓] the three main differences between dictionaries of the past and today.

1 The data sources are much more extensive than before.

2 Dictionary definitions today are based on real examples of language use.

3 More words are added to dictionaries—these include slang and technical words.

4 Dictionaries are updated much more rapidly.

5 Dictionaries now include pronunciation notes.

COMMUNICATION Talking about new words

Complete the conversation. Number the sentences (**1–7**) in the correct order.

a ______ Hmm … maybe I'll sign up for a session one of these days.

b ______ Oh, I'm attending a webinar on management studies.

c ______ Well, a webinar is a seminar that's on the Internet.

d ______ Wow, that's a cool way to study!

e ______ A what? What does that mean?

f __1__ Hey, what are you doing on Saturday?

g ______ Yeah, it is. There's a wide range of topics to choose from, and most of them are free.

9B

LANGUAGE FOCUS Describing word trends

A Complete the paragraph. Circle the correct words.

The English language [1] (**is changing** / **used to change**) all the time. One example is the usage of gender-neutral nouns for jobs. For example, in the past, people [2] (**use to** / **used to**) say *waiter* for men and *waitress* for women, but now many people say *server*, which [3] (**includes** / **included**) both men and women. Instead of *policeman* or *policewoman*, many prefer to say *police officer*. Some people are against this change because they think that these gender-specific nouns [4] (**use to** / **used to**) give us useful information about the identity of the person.

B Correct the mistakes in the sentences below.

1 We didn't used to have so many slang words years ago.

2 Did you used to send letters by post in the old days?

3 How did people used communicate over long distances in the past?

4 Some people use to send messages by radio.

5 Before the Internet, people didn't use to having access to so much information.

C Complete the sentences using your own words.

1 I ____________________ ride a bike to school. I would normally go by bus.

2 I ____________________ smoke, but not anymore.

3 Did your father ____________________ have a red car before?

4 I ____________________ go to the gym every evening, but now I hardly have time!

5 She ____________________ have many friends, but she's the most popular girl in school now!

LISTENING FOCUS Pronunciation of *used to*

A ▶ **9.2** The verb *use* is pronounced with a /z/ sound. However, when we're talking about past habits with *used to*, it is pronounced with an /s/ sound. Listen and repeat the following examples.

People **used to** write letters and send postcards. /s/

People **used** letters and postcards to keep in touch. /z/

Phones **didn't use to** have cameras in them. /s/

People **didn't use** their phones to take photos. /z/

B ▶ **9.3** Listen to five sentences. Is *use* pronounced with a /z/ or /s/ sound? Circle the sound you hear.

1 /z/ /s/

2 /z/ /s/

3 /z/ /s/

4 /z/ /s/

5 /z/ /s/

C ▶ **9.4** Listen. Circle the best response.

1 a We used to study French.

b We are studying French this semester.

2 a They're used to share pictures.

b I used to use Whatsapp and Viber.

3 a Diaries are used to record everyday experiences.

b They used to record their experiences.

4 a She plays the guitar.

b She used to play the guitar.

5 a They're used to detect cancer cells.

b They used to use nanorobots to detect cancer cells.

D ▶ **9.5** Listen and write the sentences you hear.

1 ______________________________

2 ______________________________

3 ______________________________

4 ______________________________

5 ______________________________

9C

READING

Read the passage and answer the questions.

1 Languages all over the world frequently "borrow" words from each other. Just as English words have been borrowed by other languages, English also uses a large number of foreign words. Here are some interesting ways that borrowed words are used in English.

Bungalow

2 The word *bungalow* in English is used to describe a house which has only one level. Originally from India, the word was used to described houses in the Bengali style. These houses were usually simple one-floor homes used by employees of the British trading companies. Later this style of housing was copied to make more luxurious houses for the British and then brought to England, where it is now mainly used to describe small one-story houses.

Boutique

3 This word *boutique* is borrowed from French, where it simply means a shop, but in English, it is now used to mean a small store that sells fashionable clothing or accessories. Extended meanings nowadays use the word to describe small companies that offer specialized services. A boutique hotel, for example, offers unique furnishings and services that you won't find in major hotel chains.

Robot

4 The word *robot* is used to mean an automated machine, and increasingly a machine with artificial intelligence. The word was originally invented by a Czech artist, Josef Čapek, but it was his brother, Karel Čapek, who popularized the word when he used it in his 1920 play. In the play, machines were used to replace workers and eventually took over the human race. Čapek based the word on the Czech word for "work," *robota*.

5 These are just three examples of the hundreds of borrowed words that are used in English every day.

A Which "borrowed" word mentioned in the passage ___

1 can be used to describe a kind of shop? ______________________________

2 describes the same thing in English as it does in the original language? ______________

3 was invented by an artist? ______________________________

B Circle **T** for true, **F** for false, or **NG** for not given.

1 The English language borrows many words from other languages.	**T**	**F**	**NG**
2 The word *bungalow* was originally used to describe simple one-floor homes.	**T**	**F**	**NG**
3 The word *bungalow* became widely used in Britain in the 19th century.	**T**	**F**	**NG**
4 The meaning of *boutique* has been expanded from its original definition.	**T**	**F**	**NG**
5 A boutique hotel is one that has similar hotels in different locations.	**T**	**F**	**NG**
6 The word *boutique* became popular after it was used by a famous fashion brand.	**T**	**F**	**NG**
7 The word *robot* became popular after it was used in a play.	**T**	**F**	**NG**
8 *Robota* means "machine" in Czech.	**T**	**F**	**NG**

VOCABULARY BUILDING

A Complete the sentences using the words in the box.

banned	**convey**	**noticeable**	**rapidly**	**strengthen**

1 He asked me to ______________ a message to his sister.

2 Language is ______________ evolving to reflect developments in society.

3 Some people feel that the use of slang should be ______________.

4 Language change has become more ______________ because of the Internet.

5 The introduction of new words can help ______________ the language.

B Complete the sentences with the correct form of the words in the box.

strong	**weak**	**soft**	**wide**

1 The contractors worked through the night to ______________ the narrow road.

2 She kept the butter out on the table to ______________ it.

3 The frequent floods caused the bridge to ______________.

4 She took singing lessons to ______________ her voice.

LISTENING

A ▶ **9.6** **Listen. Choose the best title for the talk.**

a Why Icelandic Is Disappearing

b How Icelanders Are Protecting Their Language

c Influences That Are Changing the Icelandic Language

B ▶ **9.6** **Listen again. Complete the table using information from the talk.**

The Problem
1 Due to the influences of globalization and the Internet, more and more people are using ______________________ words to communicate.
2 For most, this is a way for languages to ______________________, but for some, it is a ______________________ to their culture and identity.
3 The people of ______________________ are particularly concerned that their ancient language will soon disappear.
The Solution
4 The government: • set up a(n) ______________________ to protect the language. • Their role is to monitor the use of ______________________ words in ______________________ and find alternative words in their native language to say the same thing.
5 The people: • formed language committees to find ______________________ for ancient words.
The Future
6 Some people believe the best way to preserve a language is to ______________________ change, but others feel a language has to ______________________ and develop in order to stay alive.

C **Read the statements below. Circle the statement you most agree with. Give reasons to support your answer.**

a If a language does not evolve, it will eventually die out.

b Language preservation is important in preserving a culture's identity.

Reason: ______________________

____

____

9D

TED PLAYLIST

A typical text message exchange

In this fun, short talk Erin McKean encourages her audience to create new words when the existing ones won't quite do. She lists six ways to make new words in English, from compounding to "verbing," in order to make language better at expressing what we mean, and to create more ways for us to understand one another.

Patricia Ryan is an English teacher who asks a fascinating question: Is the world's focus on English preventing the spread of great ideas in other languages? She explains that when a language dies, a lot of ideas are lost as well. It's a passionate defense of translating and sharing ideas.

Does texting mean the death of good writing skills? John McWhorter suggests that texting is much more similar to speaking than to writing and finds a lot of cultural and linguistic complexity in the way texting is developing as a medium of communication.

A Match the talk title to the correct speaker.

1 Go Ahead, Make Up New Words ○	○ **a** John McWhorter
2 Don't Insist on English ○	○ **b** Erin McKean
3 Txtng Is Killing Language. JK!!! ○	○ **c** Patricia Ryan

B Which speakers most likely said the following? Circle the correct answer.

1 "If you can speak like writing, then logically it follows that you might want to also sometimes write like you speak."

a Erin McKean **b** Patricia Ryan **c** John McWhorter

2 "You should make words because every word is a chance to express your idea and get your meaning across."

a Erin McKean **b** Patricia Ryan **c** John McWhorter

3 "When a language dies, we don't know what we lose with that language."

a Erin McKean **b** Patricia Ryan **c** John McWhorter

C Decide which talk you most want to watch. Watch it online at www.ted.com.

9E

WRITING Making an argument

A Read the sample paragraph about how the use of emojis has changed language.

In the first paragraph, describe the language change.

One example of language change caused by the Internet is the use of emojis to express attitudes and emotions.

In the second paragraph, describe how it is different from the past and what people do now.

In the past, people <u>used to</u> write about their emotions using a variety of descriptive phrases. They used words to express their feelings in unique and individual ways. But nowadays, people tend to just click on an emoji and add it to their emails or their text messages.

Use some new words from this unit.

In the third paragraph, describe why some people are for or against this language change.

Some people are against this trend because they think it restricts our ability to convey emotions in language. They argue that there aren't enough emojis to match every subtle difference in feeling, so we often choose one even if it doesn't really match what we're feeling.

Personally, I am in favor of emojis, as they are quick and easy and fun, and there are new ones being invented all the time, so it's very creative, too.

In the final paragraph, state your opinion and give a reason.

B Do you think texting is degrading the English Language? Answer the questions to plan your passage.

1 What is the language change?

2 How is it different from before?

3 What are the benefits and the drawbacks?

4 What is your opinion about the change?

C Now write your passage. Then complete the checklist below.

- ☐ Did you use correct spelling and punctuation?
- ☐ Did you use some new words from this unit?
- ☐ Did you explain the language change?
- ☐ Did you state reasons for your opinion?

10 Understanding Emotions

10A

VOCABULARY Describing feelings

A Match the two parts of each sentence.

1 I sometimes feel overwhelmed when ○	○ **a** it is your first day at a new school.
2 It's normal to feel lonely when ○	○ **b** you hear bad news.
3 I tend to get frustrated when ○	○ **c** there are too many things to do at once.
4 I was delighted to hear that ○	○ **d** I can't solve a math problem.
5 I usually feel relieved when ○	○ **e** my best friend is getting married.
6 It's normal to feel shocked when ○	○ **f** I find something I was looking for.

B How would you feel in these situations? Use words from **A** or your own ideas.

1 Your best friend holds a party and doesn't invite you.

I would probably ____

2 Your co-workers organize a cake and gifts for your birthday.

____

3 You applied for a job but it's been three weeks and you haven't had a reply.

____

4 You took a driving test for the third time and passed.

____

LISTENING Dealing with emotions

A ▶ **10.1** Listen. Circle the best answer.

1 What is the conversation about?

a applying for a job **b** work stress **c** good managers

2 What is the speaker's problem?

a too much work **b** a difficult boss **c** loneliness

3 Choose the best sentence to replace "You really mustn't take it so personally."

   a You shouldn't let it affect you.

   b You really must make it your problem.

   c It's a really serious problem.

B ▶ **10.1** Listen again. Which sentence would be the most suitable ending for the conversation? Circle the best option.

   a It won't be good for you or your health in the long run.

   b It won't look good on your résumé.

   c It's nothing to worry about.

COMMUNICATION Talking about managing emotions

A Complete the conversation. Number the sentences (**1–6**) in the correct order.

   a ______ Well, I was in a hurry. I just thought sending a text message would be quicker.

   b __1__ Why didn't you reply to my text message? I need the book you borrowed to complete my assignment!

   c ______ Yeah, I do. And I'm sorry I got angry just now. It's just the stress of all these assignments.

   d ______ OK, I see. Well, I'm sorry. Do you still need it? I can come by your house later to return it.

   e ______ Hey, calm down. What text message? I'm sorry, but I don't check my phone very often. Why didn't you call me and ask for it?

   f ______ It's OK. I understand. I should have returned it sooner.

B Answer the questions using your own words.

   1 What makes you upset or angry?

   ____

   2 What do you do when you feel upset or angry?

   ____

10B

LANGUAGE FOCUS Discussing EQ and jobs

A Correct the mistakes in the sentences below.

   1 They said us we should take an EQ test.

   2 The interviewer asked to us describe a situation.

   3 The assistant promised sending us the results.

   4 According a recent study, EQ is essential in most jobs.

B ▶ **10.2** Listen. Write down what each speaker says.

1 He said ______________________

2 Our teacher reminded ______________________

3 She said that ______________________

4 He promised ______________________

C Complete the sentences. Circle the correct word.

1 My colleague (**promised** / **reminded**) to help me with my report.

2 The manager (**asked** / **told**) us if we had any problems with our team.

3 My friend (**said** / **told**) me that her boss promised them a raise.

4 The interviewer (**promised** / **reminded**) me to send a copy of my EQ test results.

LISTENING FOCUS Contraction of *would* or *had*

A ▶ **10.3** The contraction *'d* can be the short form of *would* or *had*. Notice the tense of the verb that follows *'d*. Listen and repeat what you hear.

She said she**'d apply** for another job.	(she **would**)
She said she**'d applied** for another job.	(she **had**)

B ▶ **10.4** Listen. Circle the sentence you hear.

1 **a** Did Martin say he'd sent in his application?
  b Did Martin say he'd send in his application?

2 **a** Did they ask if you'd lived overseas?
  b Did they ask if you'd live overseas?

3 **a** Did you say you'd worked as a manager?
  b Did you say you'd work as a manager?

4 **a** He said he'd study biology.
  b He said he'd studied biology.

5 **a** She asked if he'd picked up the shopping items.
  b She asked if he'd pick up the shopping items.

C ▶ **10.5** Listen. Circle the best response to each question you hear.

1 **a** Yes, I'd love to go to Paris.
  b Yes, I went to Paris last year.

2 **a** No, she's not interested in the position.
  b No, she didn't send her application in.

3 **a** Yes, he said he'd lived there for four years.
  b He said he might consider it.

4 **a** She's still thinking about it.
  b Yes, her first game was last Wednesday.

10C

READING

Read the passage and answer the questions.

1 Do you find it difficult to tell how another person is feeling? Do you feel frustrated when other people don't realize what mood you're in? Technology now has the answer: clothing and jewelry with built-in sensors that show our feelings.

Wearable technology on display at the wearable Expo in Tokyo, Japan

2 One idea is a dress that tracks your heart rate and monitors your stress level. Flashing blue lights on the dress start blinking rapidly when you feel stressed and more slowly when you feel relaxed. Designers have also come up with fabrics that change color according to your emotions. Joy, sadness, anger, and stress each have a different color.

3 Another idea is an undershirt that can transmit emotional data wirelessly to another person who can be some distance away. This undershirt has a sensor built into its sleeve. It measures your physical state and sends messages to the Internet. Those messages are then sent to another person who is wearing a necklace. The necklace lights up with different colors. This would be great for couples who want to stay in touch with their partners who may be far away, and also for parents who want to know how their children are feeling.

4 A third design concept is an emotion tracker in the form of a wristband, called *Feel*. On the inside of the wristband, there are sensors that measure skin temperature, pulse, and sweat. *Feel* collects and tracks the information and sends it to your phone in the form of a graph. You can see when your stress levels were high and what your mood was at different times of the day. It also sends suggestions about how to reduce stress and feel calmer, for example, advising you on breathing and meditation exercises.

5 Emotional awareness is an important part of how we build relationships with others. These are just some examples of how designers are coming up with creative and exciting new ideas to combine emotion and technology.

A Circle the best answer.

1 Which title best summarizes the theme of the passage?

a Devices That Make You Feel Better

b Latest Designs in the Fashion Industry

c Technology That Reads Your Emotions

2 Which sentence would be the best ending for paragraph 2?

a The result? Other people can tell right away whether it's a good idea to talk to you or whether to stay away!

b This could also be an important tool for nurses and caregivers to find out how their patients are coping with their daily lives, even when they aren't present.

c They are visible reminders to exercise, take medications, or get a better night's sleep.

B Match the description to the correct wearable device.

1 Sends your data to the Internet, and then to your partner.	o	o	**a** wristband
2 Sends data to your phone and presents it in the form of a graph.	o	o	**b** dress
3 Flashing lights indicate when you are feeling stressed.	o	o	**c** undershirt and necklace

LISTENING

A ▶ **10.6** Listen. What is the talk mainly about?

a the benefits of using emotion tracking technology at work

b why emotion tracking technology might not be as good as it sounds

c the different emotions that an emotion tracker can pick up

B ▶ **10.6** Listen again. Circle the best answer.

1 Why does the speaker mention staff meetings?

a to give an example of a situation when emotion trackers might be useful

b to explain how emotion trackers could change our behavior

c to describe a possible disadvantage of emotion trackers

2 According to the speaker, what is one thing that emotion trackers cannot do?

a give a full picture of our emotions

b measure our physical state

c communicate with people around us

3 Why does the speaker mention privacy?

a It's something that people are not so concerned about these days.

b It's a problem that technology companies are working to solve.

c It's a reason you may not want to wear an emotion tracker.

C CRITICAL THINKING

1 Do you think the speaker would use any of the wearables mentioned in the reading passage? Give reasons for your answer.

____

____

____

____

2 How do you feel about wearables that can detect and show others how you're feeling? Would you use them? Give reasons for your answer.

____

____

____

____

VOCABULARY BUILDING

A Complete the sentences using the words in the box.

combine	comfort	companion	permission	privacy

1 My best friend is a great traveling ____________. He's really fun.

2 Some robots are able to recognize human emotions. They have been designed to offer ____________ when a person is sad or unhappy.

3 She could not use the lab without first getting ____________ from her professor.

4 Some people don't like using social media because of concerns about ____________.

5 You need to ____________ the dry ingredients first before mixing them with the wet ingredients.

B Complete the sentences using the words in the box.

for	invasion	obtain	provide	with

1 It is not always possible to ____________ permission to use someone's photograph.

2 Using someone's personal data is considered a(n) ____________ of privacy.

3 Many believe pets can ____________ great comfort to people suffering from serious illness.

4 Robots can be useful companions ____________ elderly people.

5 These robots combine human characteristics ____________ mechanical features.

10D

TED PLAYLIST

A human-like robot on display in a department store in Tokyo, Japan

A LOOK INSIDE THE BRAIN IN REAL TIME

Neuroscientist and inventor Christopher deCharms demonstrates a new way to use scans to show brain activity—thoughts, emotions, and pain—while it is happening. In other words, you can actually see how you feel.

HOW WE READ EACH OTHER'S MINDS

Sensing the motives and feelings of others is a natural ability we all have, but how do we do it? Rebecca Saxe describes the discovery of a special region in the brain that we use to consider other people's thoughts. She explains that differences in this region of the brain cause people to read and judge each other differently.

ROBOTS THAT "SHOW EMOTION"

David Hanson combines robotics and art to design life-like, social robots that can imitate human expression and emotion. It is now easier for humans to interact with robots. In this talk, he gives a demonstration using a robot with a human face that looks just like Albert Einstein.

A Which speakers most likely said the following? Match the speaker to the correct quote.

1 Christopher deCharms ○
2 Rebecca Saxe ○
3 David Hanson ○

○ **a** "Although we human adults are really good at understanding other minds, we weren't always that way."
○ **b** "And it was kind of spooky, because he would say these things that just sounded like they really understood you."
○ **c** "This may shock you, but we're literally reading this person's brain."

B Complete the summaries using information from the descriptions.

1 Christopher deCharms explains how ______________________ can show how a person is feeling.
2 Rebecca Saxe explains why we ______________________ people differently.
3 David Hanson shows how robots can imitate ______________________ allowing them to interact with humans.

C Decide which talk you most want to watch. Watch it online at www.ted.com.

10E

WRITING Expressing an opinion

A Read the sample passage about an emotion-sensing device.

Write a paragraph. Start by describing your device.	One idea for a smart device is a car that can sense our emotions.	
	The purpose of this device is to make driving safer.	Say what the purpose of the device is.
Describe how it works.	It uses facial recognition technology to identify the driver's emotions. If the driver is angry or <u>frustrated</u>, the car automatically reminds the driver to calm down by speaking in a calm voice or playing some soft music.	Use some new words from this unit.
Describe situations when it could be useful.	The device can also recognize if the driver is sleepy by counting how many times they blink their eyes. If the driver seems to be falling asleep, the device will remind the driver to stay alert or stop driving.	
	Devices like this could dramatically reduce the number of car accidents.	Explain how it could improve our lives.

B Describe an emotion-sensing device for schools. Answer the questions to plan your paragraph.

1 Describe your device. What is its purpose?

2 Describe how it works.

3 Describe situations when it could be useful.

4 Describe how it would improve our lives.

C Now write your paragraph. Then complete the checklist below.

- ☐ Did you use correct spelling and punctuation?
- ☐ Did you give examples of situations when the device would be useful?
- ☐ Did you use some new words from this unit?
- ☐ Did you describe how the device would improve our lives?

11 Leaders and Thinkers

11A

VOCABULARY Doing business

A Complete the sentences using the words in the box.

career	manage	reputation	ruthless	run a company

1 A ____________________ person is very harsh or determined, and will do anything that is necessary to achieve their goal.

2 If people think you're a nice person, you have a good ____________________.

3 A ____________________ is the job or profession that someone does for a long period of time.

4 If you ____________________, you have to ____________________ the staff and oversee all aspects of the business.

B Answer the questions.

1 If you had the chance to start a business, what kind of business would it be? Why?

____

2 What is the biggest risk you've taken in your life?

____

LISTENING Starting a business

A ▶ 11.1 Listen. What is the talk about?

a reasons to start an online business

b ways to make money online

c how to make your online business a success

B ▶ 11.1 Listen again. Check [✓] the advice given by the speaker.

1 ☐ determine market needs

2 ☐ attend to customer complaints immediately

3 ☐ create an interesting website for your product

4 ☐ look for creative ways to market your product

5 ☐ think carefully about pricing

COMMUNICATION: Talking about what makes a good leader

A Complete the conversation. Number the sentences (**1–7**) in the correct order.

a __1__ Hey, can I ask you a question? I'm working on a project and I need some help.

b ____ Well, what do you think are the characteristics of a good leader?

c ____ OK. Yeah, I agree. Can you think of anything else?

d ____ Sure, how can I help?

e ____ Hmmm, I think a good leader should be decisive.

f ____ Yeah, communication is really important. Thanks for your help!

g ____ I think they also need to be good communicators.

B Answer the questions using your own words.

1 What characteristics do you think are necessary for a leader to have?

____

2 Do you think you would make a good leader? Why?

____

____

11B

LANGUAGE FOCUS What makes a CEO?

A Rewrite each sentence using either *should, need to, have to,* or *must.*

1 It's a good idea for employees to have flexible working hours.

Employees ____

2 It's not necessary for staff members to have meetings every day.

Staff members ____

3 It's essential for managers to be good communicators.

Managers ____

4 It's very important not to have fixed ideas about how to do things.

You ____

5 It's not a good idea for managers to be too authoritarian.

Managers ____

B Complete the sentences using your own words.

1 ______________________________ be on time for work.

2 ______________________________ polite and respectful to their classmates.

3 The English club members ______________________________.

4 Weekly assignments ______________________________.

5 Students ______________________________.

6 Employees ______________________________.

C ▶ **11.2** Listen to the statements. Is each speaker talking about an obligation or giving advice? Circle the correct answer.

1 **a** talking about an obligation **b** giving advice

2 **a** talking about an obligation **b** giving advice

3 **a** talking about an obligation **b** giving advice

4 **a** talking about an obligation **b** giving advice

5 **a** talking about an obligation **b** giving advice

LISTENING FOCUS Linking sounds

A ▶ **11.3** When a word ends in a vowel sound and the next word starts with a vowel sound, we introduce an extra sound to make the transition smoother. Listen to these sentences and repeat the linking sounds.

You must be $_y$ able to recruit the right people.
We should meet for coffee $_y$ and discuss the plan.

Do $_w$ I have to work this weekend?
Things may not go $_w$ according to plan.

B ▶ **11.4** Circle the words that are linked, and write *w* or *y* between the words. Then listen and check your answers.

1 You shouldn't be afraid of taking risks.

2 Even if the odds are against you, you should do it.

3 Leaders need to inspire people.

4 You need to be ambitious.

5 People with no experience of business may find it hard.

6 You only realize your mistakes afterwards.

C ▶ **11.5** Listen to the phrases. Circle the linking sound you hear.

1 **a** y **b** w

2 **a** y **b** w

3 **a** y **b** w

4 **a** y **b** w

5 **a** y **b** w

11C

READING

Read the passage and answer the questions.

What does it take to be successful? It turns out that being ready to fail may be an important factor. Successful people aren't discouraged by failure. They see failure as an opportunity to learn from their mistakes. Whatever happens, they don't give up.

James Dyson owns a multimillion-dollar company that sells vacuum cleaners and hand dryers. In 1978, while vacuuming his home, James Dyson realized his vacuum cleaner wasn't working well. So he decided to design a new one that was more powerful and efficient. He designed over 5,000 prototypes and after thousands of failed designs, he finally succeeded. However, manufacturers didn't want to take on his design. He took a risk and decided to form his own company to market the product. Now it has a reputation as one of the best vacuum cleaners in the world.

James Dyson

Stephen King is a best-selling author who has written over 50 novels, many of which have been turned into movies. He has sold over 350 million copies of his works. However, at the beginning of his career, he received hundreds of rejection letters from publishers who wouldn't consider his work. King's first novel, *Carrie*, was rejected 30 times. King actually threw the manuscript away, but it was later rescued by his wife. *Carrie* was King's first successful novel and marked the beginning of his remarkable career.

Stephen King

Oprah Winfrey is a billionaire who owns a huge media production company and is one of the most popular and well-known talk show hosts. But the start of her media career wasn't very promising. She was hired as the co-host of a TV show, but the show wasn't successful and she was dropped after a few months. She was given reporting assignments, but her bosses said she was too personally involved to be a good reporter. Yet it is her empathy and personal approach that makes her the success she is today.

Oprah Winfrey

A What do the three people mentioned in the passage have in common?

a They failed before they succeeded.

b They are famous people who achieved instant success.

c They all invented a product that became very famous.

B Complete the summary. Circle the correct words.

James Dyson wanted to create a vacuum cleaner that 1 (**was cheaper** / **worked better**) than the one he owned. Many of his inventions were unsuccessful and nobody wanted to sell them. He finally achieved success by 2 (**approaching a rich investor** / **forming his own company**).

Stephen King received many rejection letters at the start of his career. The manuscript for his first novel, *Carrie*, was rejected so many times that he 3 (**gave up writing** / **threw it away**). Fortunately, thanks to his wife, it later became King's 4 (**first** / **most**) successful novel.

Oprah Winfrey is a 5 (**talk show host** / **writer**) who did not have a promising start early in her career. Her bosses thought she was too 6 (**caring** / **talkative**). It is that very same character that has made her a success today.

C Use the information (**a–f**) to complete the Venn diagram.

a experienced failure before achieving success

b owns a big company

c developed many prototypes before coming up with a working model

d the cause of their initial failure was the reason for their later success

e nobody wanted to market their work

f became successful after taking a risk

Stephen King James Dyson

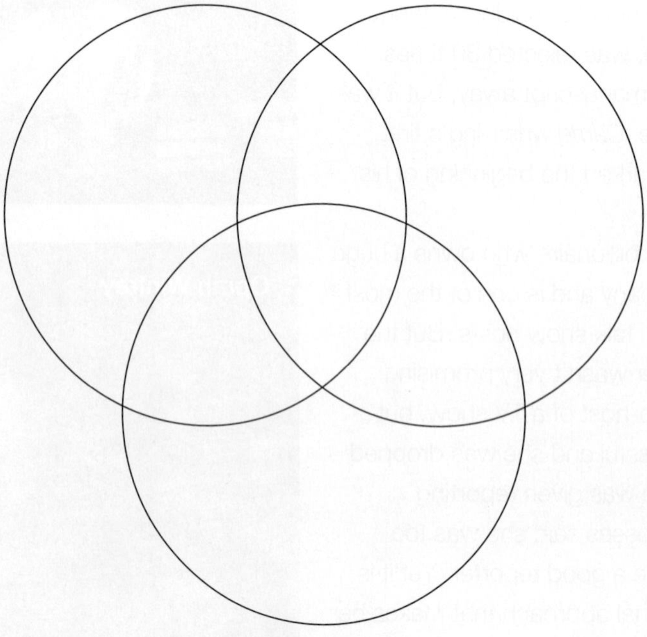

Oprah Winfrey

LISTENING

A ▶ **11.6** Listen. What is the main theme of the talk?

a how to keep going when faced with failure

b how to succeed in everything you do

c how to deal with criticism from others

B ▶ **11.6** Listen again. Number the advice (**1–4**) in the order that you hear it. One is extra.

a ______ Find ways to refine your ideas.

b ______ Find a friend to help you.

c ______ Make the most of your strengths.

d ______ Don't be afraid to try something new.

e ______ Believe in yourself.

C **CRITICAL THINKING** Which advice in **B** (**a–e**) do you think applies most to each person in the passage?

1 James Dyson ______

2 Stephen King ______

3 Oprah Winfrey ______

VOCABULARY BUILDING

A Complete the sentences. Circle the correct option.

1 Your **principles** are ______.

a facts about your life **b** values that influence your behavior

2 If you **win** someone **over**, you ______.

a beat them easily **b** persuade them to support you

3 If you **took action**, it means you ______ something.

a did **b** did not do

4 If you are **on the lookout** for something, it means you are ______.

a searching for it **b** hiding from it

5 If someone makes a **pledge**, they make a serious ______ to do something.

a effort **b** promise

B Check [✓] the verbs that can be used with the word *action*.

☐ take ☐ make ☐ call for ☐ put into

11D

TED PLAYLIST

A group of colleagues enjoying time away from the office

HOW TO MANAGE FOR COLLECTIVE CREATIVITY

Harvard professor Linda Hill spent many years studying the behavior of innovative leaders working in 12 different industries. Based on her research, she's developed a set of tools and techniques to keep great ideas flowing from everyone in the company.

HOW TO RUN A COMPANY WITH (ALMOST) NO RULES

CEO Ricardo Semler doesn't make his employees report the number of holidays they take, and he invites workers to join the company's board. He also allows workers to choose a shorter working week for less pay. Why? Because he trusts them to do a good job, and believes happy people make better workers.

WHY GOOD LEADERS MAKE YOU FEEL SAFE

What makes a great leader? Management theorist Simon Sinek suggests it's someone who makes their employees feel secure, who draws workers into a circle of trust. But creating trust and safety—especially in an uneven economy—means taking on big responsibility.

A What is the theme of the playlist? Circle the best answer.

a creating trust in the workplace **b** advice for business leaders **c** helping people be creative

B Circle the correct answer.

1 Which sentence is true about Linda Hill?

a She runs a company where ideas are actively encouraged.

b She has developed ways to help companies encourage creativity.

c Her ideas are based on her experience working as a CEO.

2 Ricardo Semler allows his employees to choose a shorter working week because ____.

a it reduces costs **b** he trusts them **c** it improves creativity

3 Which two speakers have a similar style for dealing with employees?

a Semler and Sinek **b** Hill and Sinek **c** Hill and Semler

C Decide which talk you most want to watch. Watch it online at www.ted.com.

11E

WRITING Describing your business style

A Read the sample passage about a leader's business philosophy.

Write one paragraph. Start by describing your guiding principles.	My business philosophy would be based on the values of creativity, respect, and fairness. The way I would run a company would be to allow my employees to express their creativity and ideas. I would ask all employees to contribute their ideas on how best to run the company. In addition, I would offer them training and professional development and good career prospects.	Then explain how another one of these principles works in practice and give an example.
Use some new words from this unit.	I would like my company to have a good <u>reputation</u> for treating employees in a fair and friendly way. People are the most valuable resource in a company, so I think it's important to create an environment where they can feel they are doing their best.	Conclude by summing up your ideas.

B Imagine you are a business leader. Describe your company's business philosophy, how you would run your company, and what kinds of employees you would want. Answer the questions to plan your paragraph.

1 What principles are the company's philosophy based on?

2 Explain how these principles work in practice and give an example for each.

3 Describe the kind of employees you look for.

4 Conclude by summing up your ideas.

C Now write your paragraph. Then complete the checklist below.

- ☐ Did you use correct spelling and punctuation?
- ☐ Did you use some new words from this unit?
- ☐ Did you describe your guiding principles?
- ☐ Did you describe how they will work in practice by giving examples?

12 Well-being

12A

VOCABULARY Describing health and well-being

A Complete the paragraph using the words in the box.

recharge	strengthen	stressful	work-life balance

If you work long hours in a [1] ________________ job, it's important to take time off to relax and [2] ________________ your batteries. Try to stay active throughout the day and avoid sitting for long periods of time. Eating plenty of fresh fruit and vegetables, will [3] ________________ your immune system. People who take regular breaks tend to be more productive in their work and handle problems more easily. When you go home, try not to check your work emails or messages. Achieving a good [4] ________________ will help you stay healthy and stress-free.

B Complete the sentences using your own words.

1 I try not to include too much ________________________________ in my diet.

2 I find it ________________________________ to work late at night.

3 I stay active by ________________________________.

4 I recharge by going on vacation every ________________________________.

5 I find it easier to handle pressure at work if I ________________________________.

LISTENING What your brain does when you sleep

A ▶ **12.1** Listen. What is the talk about?

a techniques to sleep better **b** reasons for not being able to sleep **c** why we need enough sleep

B ▶ **12.1** Listen again. Circle **T** for true or **F** for false.

1	People with insomnia have trouble sleeping.	**T**	**F**
2	As we get older, we are less likely to be affected by insomnia.	**T**	**F**
3	Eating meals late at night can help you get to sleep.	**T**	**F**
4	Research shows that children sleep less if they have a TV or computer in their bedroom.	**T**	**F**
5	Stress is one of the most common causes of insomnia.	**T**	**F**

COMMUNICATION Talking about lifestyles

A Complete the conversation. Number the sentences (**1–6**) in the correct order.

a __1__ Hey, are you okay? You look tired.
b ______ I guess you're right. I should change my habits and try to go to bed earlier.
c ______ Yeah, I'm exhausted. I haven't been getting enough sleep.
d ______ Yeah, that's definitely not enough. You need at least seven to eight hours of sleep.
e ______ Um … I only got about three or four hours, I think.
f ______ How come? How much sleep did you get last night?

B Answer the questions using your own words.

1 How much sleep do you usually get every night?

____

2 What do you do to stay active?

____

3 How do you cope with stress?

____

12B

LANGUAGE FOCUS Discussing facts about sleep

A Choose the correct words to complete the sentences.

1 If you (**didn't** / **wouldn't**) drink so much coffee, you (**slept** / **would sleep**) better.
2 People (**were** / **would be**) happier if they (**had** / **would have**) a better work-life balance.
3 If I (**didn't** / **wouldn't**) work so late, I (**did** / **would do**) some exercise at the gym.
4 There (**wasn't** / **wouldn't be**) so much pollution if we all (**stopped** / **would stop**) using cars.
5 If we (**went** / **would go**) for a walk every day, we (**felt** / **would feel**) calmer and healthier.
6 If he (**weren't** / **wouldn't be**) so busy at work, he (**felt** / **wouldn't feel**) so stressed.

B Complete the sentences with your own ideas.

1 If I had more free time, ______________________________.
2 I'd be healthier if ______________________________.
3 If I were more active, ______________________________.
4 If I didn't have so much work, ______________________________.
5 I'd feel happier if ______________________________.

C ▶ **12.2** Listen to the statements. Circle the correct option.

1 a He has 3 million dollars. **b** He doesn't have 3 million dollars.

2 a She is traveling the world. **b** She wants to travel the world.

3 a He goes surfing every week. **b** He does not live by the sea.

4 a The listener should look for a new place to live. **b** The speaker is looking for a new place to live.

LISTENING FOCUS *Will* and *would*

A ▶ **12.3** It's important to be able to notice the difference between *will* and *would*. This will help distinguish if someone is talking about a likely or unlikely situation. Listen and repeat what you hear.

What **will** you do with the money?	(likely situation)
What **would** you do with the money?	(unlikely situation)
I think I'**ll** spend it on a new car.	(likely situation)
I think I'**d** spend it on a new car.	(unlikely situation)

B ▶ **12.4** Listen. Circle the words you hear.

1 How (**will** / **would**) you feel?

2 Where do you think (**you'll** / **you'd**) go?

3 (**I'll** / **I'd**) probably take the train.

4 (**I'll** / **I'd**) be really surprised.

5 (**He'll** / **He'd**) be a great manager.

6 (**It'll** / **It'd**) cost about a million dollars.

7 I think (**she'll** / **she'd**) be really upset.

8 Do you think (**it'll** / **it'd**) work?

C ▶ **12.5** Listen and write the sentences you hear.

1 ______________________________

2 ______________________________

3 ______________________________

4 ______________________________

5 ______________________________

12C

READING

Read the passage and answer the questions.

1 Finding a balance between work and life is a challenge for many people today. Should we give priority to our work, and devote ourselves to earning more money? Or should we value our family, our friends, and our leisure time more highly? Is there a way to balance work and free time in a healthy way? Let's look at two countries where people seem to have found a solution to this problem.

In some countries, governments are actively encouraging a healthy work-life balance, allowing workers to spend more time with their families.

2 Denmark is a country that frequently tops the list of the Organization for Economic Co-operation and Development (OECD) Better Life Index. Denmark has the best work-life balance of the 20 OECD countries surveyed. Only two percent of workers say they work very long hours. Danish workers work an average of 33 hours a week and have a right to at least five weeks of paid vacation each year. Danes have a high degree of flexibility at work and are often able to choose when they start their working day or when to work from home. New parents receive up to 52 weeks of government-paid parental leave. 32 of these 52 weeks are shared between the father and mother.

3 Spain is a country that also often gets a high score on the index. The survey found that Spanish people in full-time work spend 16 hours of each day on non-work activities, such as sleeping, eating, and socializing with friends. Only six percent work an average of 50 hours or more a week. Workers get 30 days paid annual vacation, plus 12 national holidays. They can have 16 weeks paid maternity leave and 15 days of paternity leave.

4 Finding the right work-life balance is different for everyone, but the lifestyles in these two countries may give us some clues as to how to maintain a balance that allows us time to value our friends and family as much as our work.

A Choose the best title for the passage.

a Countries Leading the Way in Creating Work-Life Balance

b How to Create a Work-Life Balance for Employees

c The Impact of Work-Life Balance on Families around the World

B Use the information (**a–f**) to complete the Venn diagram.

a Only 2 in 100 people say they work long hours.

b Workers are given 16 weeks of paid maternity leave.

c Fathers can take time off after the birth of a child.

d Workers can easily work from home if they choose to.

e Workers get more than four weeks of paid annual vacation.

f Example of a country with good work-life balance.

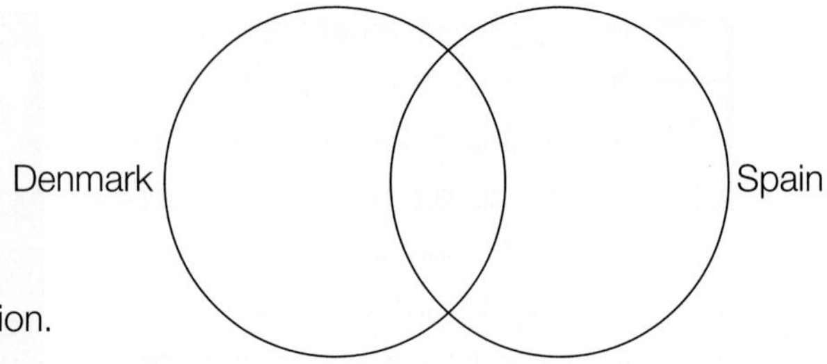

LISTENING

A ▶ **12.6** Listen. What is the main idea of the talk?

People in Singapore and South Korea ___.

a work shorter days than people in other Asian countries

b find it difficult to achieve a good work-life balance

c often work from home so they can spend time with their children

B ▶ **12.6** Listen again. Circle the correct answer.

1 Which country has the longest average working hours?

a Singapore **b** South Korea **c** Denmark

2 Why does the speaker mention Denmark?

a Parents have more time with their children.

b People in Denmark are efficient workers.

c Danish people have understanding bosses.

3 Why do some employers in Singapore dislike employees working from home?

a They think the company will look bad to its customers.

b They think working in the office is more productive.

c They think workers should meet together often.

C CRITICAL THINKING Check [✓] each box to show if the statement refers to the countries described in the passage (Denmark and Spain) or to those in the talk (Singapore and South Korea).

	Denmark and Spain	Singapore and S. Korea
1 Companies have traditional attitudes to work.	☐	☐
2 People work long hours and don't have time to start families.	☐	☐
3 Government policy helps people have a better work–life balance.	☐	☐
4 The government would like companies to change their culture.	☐	☐
5 On an average workday, people can spend more time with their family.	☐	☐
6 Companies are flexible about working hours.	☐	☐

VOCABULARY BUILDING

A Complete the paragraph with the words in the box.

flexibility	**formula**	**guilty**	**implemented**	**satisfaction**

When asked about their level of job [1] ____________________, many people say they enjoy their work but feel [2] ____________________ about not spending more time with their families. Recently, some companies have [3] ____________________ new policies with more [4] ____________________ concerning working hours and working from home. One [5] ____________________ that has worked in some organizations is to allow employees to choose their working hours, and to work from home—as long as they get their projects done on time.

B Complete the sentences with the correct form of the word *satisfy.*

satisfaction: *n.* a feeling of accomplishment

satisfactory: *adj.* adequate or acceptable

satisfied: *adj.* pleased or contented

satisfy: *v.* to fulfill a need or requirement

1 Our manager is so critical of our work that it is difficult to ____________________ her.

2 People usually get a lot of ____________________ from a job that they enjoy.

3 She left a big tip for the waiter because she was ____________________ with the service.

4 I left my job because the salary wasn't ____________________.

12D

TED PLAYLIST

THE POWER OF TIME OFF

Every seven years, designer Stefan Sagmeister closes his New York studio for a year off work, to renew his creative energy. He explains the value of time off and shows some of the projects that he developed as a result of his break on the island of Bali in Indonesia.

THE HAPPY SECRET TO BETTER WORK

In this fast-moving and very funny talk, psychologist Shawn Achor argues that, actually, happiness inspires us to be more productive. His research shows that raising somebody's level of positivity helps that person perform significantly better than when they are negative, neutral, or stressed.

GOT A MEETING? TAKE A WALK

Researchers have found evidence that sitting for long periods of time can damage your health. Nilofer Merchant suggests a small idea that just might have a big impact on your life and health: Next time you have a one-on-one meeting, make it into a "walking meeting"—and let ideas flow while you walk and talk.

A What is the theme of the playlist? Circle the best answer.

a increasing productivity **b** having fun **c** solving problems

B Which speakers most likely said the following? Circle the correct answer.

1 "We've found there are ways that you can train your brain to be able to become more positive."

a Stefan Sagmeister **b** Shawn Achor **c** Nilofer Merchant

2 "There's this amazing thing about actually getting out of the box that leads to out-of-the-box thinking. Whether it's nature or the exercise itself, it certainly works."

a Stefan Sagmeister **b** Shawn Achor **c** Nilofer Merchant

3 "I thought it might be helpful to basically cut off five of those retirement years and intersperse them in between those working years."

a Stefan Sagmeister **b** Shawn Achor **c** Nilofer Merchant

C Decide which talk you most want to watch. Watch it online at www.ted.com.

12E

WRITING Making suggestions

A Read the sample passage about an idea to increase student productivity.

Write one paragraph. Start by describing your main idea.	In my opinion, the best way to improve students' level of achievement is to implement more <u>flexibility</u> in learning.	Use some new words from this unit.
Then give some examples of how this will work.	If I could, I'd like to be able to plan my own schedule at school. Students shouldn't always have to be in class for lessons. Instead, they could choose to join lessons online, at any place and time throughout the school day. Personally, I find it easier to learn in the morning, so I'd plan my most important lessons at that time.	
	Although the school day would be longer, this way students would have time in between lessons to engage in non-academic activities.	Include one disadvantage.
Use sentences with *if*.	If students had more control over their class schedule, they would feel more motivated and get more satisfaction from their studies.	Describe the main advantage.

B Think about an idea for increasing worker productivity. Answer the questions to plan your paragraph.

1 What is your main idea for increasing productivity?

2 Give some examples of how it will work.

3 What is one disadvantage?

4 What is the main advantage?

C Now write your paragraph. Then complete the checklist below.

- ☐ Did you use correct spelling and punctuation?
- ☐ Did you use some new words from this unit?
- ☐ Did you include one disadvantage?
- ☐ Did you use sentences with *if*?

Audio Scripts

▶ 1.1 In today's podcast, we're going to look at three easy ways for companies to encourage employees to become volunteers.

The best way to encourage volunteering at work is to offer paid time for volunteering. This could mean that employees can take one day per month—or more—and donate their time as a volunteer without losing any of their salary. This shows that a company really cares about volunteering and considers it an important use of employees' time.

Another thing companies can do is to compile a list of volunteer organizations and charities that need help. You can make sure that these organizations fit with your company profile and at the same time offer employees more information and choices to choose from.

Finally, an important part of any volunteer program is to recognize and value the work that volunteers have done. Publish an article about them in the company newsletter, or organize a special lunch to acknowledge those who have volunteered.

Any or all of these strategies will have an enormous impact on the way volunteering is seen in the company and will inspire people to continue working there. Volunteering is a way to help people develop new skills and learn to get along with each other. This allows them to work better as a team, and makes a positive impact on the local community.

▶ 1.2 What do you do as a volunteer?; Whaddaya do as a volunteer?; What did you do as a volunteer?; Whadidja do as a volunteer?

▶ 1.3 **1.** What kind of work did you do?; **2.** How did you get to work?; **3.** Who do you ask for help?; **4.** What do you like about being a volunteer?

▶ 1.4 **1.** Where do you work?; **2.** Do you enjoy working there?; **3.** What did you help them with?; **4.** Do you have people to help you?

▶ 1.5 Charities that work to end poverty and hunger in developing countries have to make sure that the money reaches the people who need it most. However, they also have to make sure that the money has a long-term impact on these people.

That's what a charity called Heifer International does. Heifer International was founded over 70 years ago by Dan West—a farmer from the United States. Instead of giving money and food to communities, Heifer International donates animals—cows, sheep, water buffalo, chickens, and even bees—to families so that communities can learn to manage their own food source. The organization trains people on how to take care of these animals and how to use them to make wool, cheese, or honey.

An important part of the project is that whenever an animal gives birth, the family that owns it has to give the first female baby animal to another poor family and help them learn how to take care of it. This way, the knowledge and skills are passed on throughout the community and keep growing.

The ultimate goal of Heifer international is to end world hunger by creating communities around the world that have their own sustainable food sources.

▶ 2.1 Since the rise of the Internet in the 1990s, blogs have become a popular way for people to express their views on different topics to a much wider audience than ever before.

Blogging started to become popular after the first blogging websites were launched in 1999. The same year also saw the first use of the word "blog"—a short form of the word "weblog." Shortly after, the verb "to blog" and the noun "blogger" also became commonly used in English.

Since the turn of the century, many different types of blogs have arisen. Many people keep personal blogs that serve as a kind of online diary. Other blogs focus on a particular subject such as cars, technology, or fashion. According to Google, music is the most common topic for blogs like these. Many companies also have blogs, either for internal communication, or often as a way of marketing their products or services to customers.

Estimates suggest that there are now around 150 million blogs on the Internet, and the number is increasing. It's thought that two new blogs are created somewhere in the world every second!

▶ **2.2** Do you think life in the future will be **better**, or **worse**?; Do you think robots will make life **easier**, or more **difficult**?

▶ **2.3** **1.** Do you think people will have **more** free time, or **less**?; **2.** Will cities become **larger**, or **smaller**? **3.** Do you think air travel will be **faster**, or **just the same**? **4.** Will the world population **increase**, or **decrease**?

▶ **2.4** Today's podcast is all about fashion! How do fashion trends get started and who ultimately influences what we buy and wear?

A lot of fashion trends start on the street. That's right, they're styles that are worn by ordinary people who have an innovative idea—whether it's a new kind of hairstyle—or a new way to layer t-shirts. Other people notice them and start to copy their style. Street style often ends up being copied by the big fashion designers!

Another big influence is fashion bloggers. Talented fashion bloggers have their own unique styles. They take photos of themselves wearing different clothes and accessories and post the photos online. They can often develop a huge audience. Italian fashion blogger Chiara Ferragni, for example, has more than 3 million Instagram followers.

With the rise of social media, people's fashion is also becoming increasingly influenced by their friends and social peer groups. It's become so much easier to share a picture of your latest fashion idea with friends instantly. A new style idea can go viral in just a few minutes and be shared with thousands of people in just a few hours.

There's no doubt that fashion today is far more varied than ever before. People look for inspiration from a wide range of sources. As social media tools enable us to express ourselves and develop our own unique style, more and more people are becoming trendsetters, not just trend followers.

▶ **3.1** Medical technology is improving all the time. But is it possible that one day our doctors and nurses will be entirely replaced by machines? Doctors already make heavy use of computers. Computers can scan and analyze huge quantities of patients' data in a very short time and come up with a diagnosis. Some believe that this technology could be developed further. A medical robot could perform a series of routine tests on a patient, such as checking blood pressure, and then recommend a treatment. This could be especially useful for patients who visit the doctor regularly with a chronic condition such as heart disease. The human doctor would then have more time to specialize in illnesses that are more difficult to treat.

Many believe, however, that robots could never completely replace human doctors. Only humans have the ability to include emotional and psychological factors in their assessment of a patient's condition. What's more, dealing with patients' anxieties and worries about a condition is thought to be a key part of a doctor's role. It's unlikely that robots could ever provide the counseling and emotional support that human doctors can.

▶ **3.2** **1. A:** When do you usually play tennis? **B:** I usually play tennis on **Sundays**.; **2. A:** What do you usually do on Sundays? **B:** I usually **play tennis** on Sundays.

▶ **3.3** **1. A:** When are you having lunch with Daniel? **B:** I'm having lunch with him **tomorrow**.; **2. A:** Who are you having lunch with tomorrow? **B:** I'm having lunch with **Daniel** tomorrow.; **3. A:** Are you having dinner with Daniel tomorrow? **B:** No. I'm having **lunch** with him tomorrow.

▶ **3.4** **1.** What do you usually eat for breakfast?; **2.** When do you go to the gym?; **3.** Who bought you that watch?; **4.** What did the doctor tell you?

▶ **3.5** As wearable tech devices become more and more popular, there's an increasing number of devices that aim to help people with health conditions.

One of these is a wearable sensor patch that you can attach to your arm like a small adhesive bandage. The sensor collects data about your overall health, such as how many hours you sleep, what your heart rate is, and how fast you are breathing. It can also collect data from the sweat on the surface of your skin and can tell you about your blood sugar level, or whether you are drinking enough water. It can send you a summary of this data or send it to your doctor or caregiver.

The sensor is very useful for people with heart diseases, or people who have problems with high cholesterol. It can be used by patients recovering from strokes, or surgeries. It is also useful for monitoring elderly people at home to make sure they are coping well with medication.

However, it is also useful for healthy people who want to monitor their health and prevent conditions such as heart disease or diabetes.

▶ 4.1 Keeping your website fresh and up-to-date needn't be a chore! Here are some easy tips on how to improve your website.

The first thing to look at is the way you use headings to focus attention on the main information. You can make information stand out by using headings in different fonts and colors. But don't overload! Too many different styles of fonts and colors will be confusing, and users will soon give up and go to another page.

The second thing to look at is the images. Are they fresh and exciting? People who frequently visit your page don't want to see the same picture every time. Try changing the images once a month so that the page always looks fresh. There are many websites that offer hundreds of photos, many of which are free.

Finally, think about using icons for the key functions on your website. Icons immediately attract the eye and make the page look exciting and fun. You can use icons for functions such as "download" or "add to your shopping basket." There are several websites where you can download free icons. Using icons will make your website look professional and easy to navigate.

These small design tweaks can help to refresh your website and keep users interested in visiting your website again!

▶ 4.2 This computer is faster and easier to use than other models. More and more are people going online to compare products.

▶ 4.3 **1.** The best feature is the sound quality.; **2.** There were other headphones in the review.; **3.** I'm looking for a cheap but stylish pair.; **4.** These headphones are good for outdoor use.; **5.** Each product received an overall score out of ten. **6.** This one is more expensive than the others.

▶ 4.4

M: How's your new computer? Is it better than your old one?

W: It's faster and easier to use! I bought it online.

M: Really? Is it cheaper online?

W: Yes, it's more expensive to buy one in a store.

M: Wow! I never knew that. I should look online more often!

▶ 4.5

W: Hey, Greg! Did you manage to find those new headphones online? Did you buy them?

M: Hi Tina! Well yes and no. Yes, I found them online, but no I didn't buy them.

W: You didn't! Why not?

M: Well ... there were a couple of different reasons. I managed to find the site and it looked very professional—amazing photos and clear descriptions for all their products. It was easy to use the search box to find the headphones I was looking for, so I found the ones I wanted. But when I clicked on the "buy now" button, I had to fill out this really long form with all sorts of personal information like my birth date, annual income, and so on.

W: Oh no, that's really frustrating. That's how you end up getting lots of spam.

M: Right! And this made me a bit suspicious, you know, why would they need all this information from me? So I started to look around the site more carefully, and I couldn't find any contact information. What if I sent them my money, and I didn't get my headphones—who would I contact?

W: You're right, that is kind of scary. You should send them a complaint.

M: Hah! That's another thing. There was no way to ask a question or send in a complaint because there was no feedback form or contact information!

W: Hmm...You were right not to buy your headphones from them.

▶ 5.1

M: Have you heard about this new urban gardening association?

W: No, what is it?

M: Well, a group of residents are getting together to start urban gardens on the roofs of buildings and train stations. There'll be quite a large number of small plots available and anyone who lives in the area can apply to get one.

W: Oh really? So you can grow your own vegetables and flowers and that type of thing?

M: Exactly! Wouldn't it be great to have home-grown vegetables for your dinner?

W: Wow! That does sound good. I really miss having my own backyard in the city.

M: Yeah, there are so many benefits from this project. It's a really good way to create more greenery in the city.

W: … and it'll help reduce pollution!

M: You're absolutely right! Plus, it's not just about growing your own food, it's also about building a community so people can learn from each other and help each other.

W: That would be a great way to meet people and make friends. Maybe I could join?

M: Sure! There's a meeting about it at the library this weekend—let's go there together!

▶ **5.2** A bridge can be constructed.; The walls can't be painted.; The river can be cleaned.; The streets can't be repaired.

▶ **5.3** **1.** The water can't be used.; **2.** Trees can be planted.; **3.** It can be improved.; **4.** A sports center can be built.; **5.** They can't be replaced.

▶ **5.4** **1.** This trash can be recycled.; **2.** You can't park here.; **3.** I can't understand what you're saying.; **4.** He can help with the project.; **5.** The park can't be built until summer.

▶ **5.5** Washed Ashore is an art exhibition at the Smithsonian's National Zoo in Washington, D.C. It is designed to raise awareness of how much trash we are throwing into our oceans.

Seen from a distance, these massive sculptures look like brightly colored sea creatures—larger-than-life fish, seals, and jellyfish. But look at them more closely, and you'll be surprised.

The sculptures are entirely made out of trash that has been washed ashore onto our beaches—plastic bottles, plastic bags, containers,and old toothbrushes, amongst many other things.

The project was started by Angela Pozzi, an artist and educator based in Bandon, Oregon. She is dedicated to reducing trash in our oceans. She wants to attract people's attention with the beauty of the sculptures, which then become horrifying as you get close up. It was a real community project. She recruited volunteers to collect trash from the beach and then build the sculptures together.

There are 143 billion kilograms of plastic in the world's oceans, and trash is found everywhere—even on beaches in Alaska. This poses a significant danger to wildlife. When birds or seals eat plastic, they can choke on it and die. When fish eat plastic, it poisons them. This poison is then passed on up the food chain to larger fish and ultimately to us when we eat fish. This art exhibition motivates us all to do more to reduce trash in our oceans.

▶ **6.1** If you're a manager, effective communication is the key to success. Having clear communication will help your team work together effectively, prevent misunderstandings, and ensure your projects run more smoothly. Here are three tips to help you communicate effectively with your team.

First, use different communication channels. Holding a group meeting is fine, and may seem time-efficient, but it is important to remember that some people respond better to individual communication, such as emails and one-to-one meetings. Try to notice which channels work best with which people.

Second, use a tone that creates a relaxed and supportive atmosphere. Although some managers use a more commanding tone, this can sometimes hurt their employees' feelings and cause resentment. Try to use a tone that is friendly but assertive. Avoid sarcasm, and always show a willingness to listen. This will make team members feel involved and more willing to contribute their creative ideas.

And finally, it's important to show that you appreciate your team's efforts and that you are aware of their contributions. If you have a meeting, always thank your staff for their time. If someone contributes a good idea, make sure you praise them for it. This will demonstrate that you are open to ideas and will encourage others to give their opinions, too.

▶ 6.2

M: I really don't like group meetings.

W: Really? I find them really useful.

M: I really don't like group meetings.

W: Yeah. They can be really boring.

▶ 6.3 **1. M:** Email is so old-fashioned. **W:** Yeah. I never use it these days.; **2. W:** I really don't like using Facebook. **M:** Really? I use it every day.; **3. M:** I hate speaking in public. **W:** Yeah? I actually quite enjoy it.

▶ 6.4 **1.** I thought it was really interesting.; **2.** I thought it was too short.; **3.** I found the end part the most interesting.; **4.** Her delivery was really good.

▶ 6.5

M: I quite enjoyed that presentation.

W: Yeah. I thought it was really interesting.

M: It was a bit too long though.

W: Did you think so? I thought it was too short.

M: Really? You didn't get bored near the end. I know I did.

W: No. I found the end part the most interesting.

M: Okay. She was a great speaker though.

W: Yeah. Her delivery was really good.

▶ 6.6 "Lab Girl" is a book about plant science, written by Hope Jahren—a professor of geobiology at the University of Hawaii. The book is a fascinating account of her life as a plant biologist and gives readers an insight into the amazing world of plants. Jahren uses language that inspires and awakens curiosity. Every page conveys her own passion and enthusiasm.

Jahren starts by asking the reader to look out of the window and look for something green. If you see a leaf, she says, it is most probably a type that has been around for more than four million years. The author then asks the reader a series of questions about the leaf, before prompting the reader to ask a question of their own. Using this technique, she brings her audience into the world of plant science—because asking questions about a leaf, tree, or plant, is what plant science is all about.

Jahren goes on to tell her story—of her childhood in rural Minnesota, of her fascination with the world of plants, and her struggles in her career. She contrasts the daily routine of work in the lab—often boring and exhausting—against the moments of amazing excitement when she discovers something totally new. There are scientific descriptions of plants, trees, and flowers that are concise and easy-to-understand, and at the same time vivid and beautiful. She looks at the world from the plant's point of view and compares her own human struggle with the struggle of plants to survive. At the end of the book, she encourages her readers to plant a tree.

▶ 7.1 London is one of the most multicultural cities in the world. Over eight million people from a wide range of ethnic backgrounds call it home.

One ethnic group that has contributed greatly to Britain's multicultural sense of identity came from the West Indies. In the 1950s, many people from Jamaica, Trinidad, and other Caribbean islands migrated to Britain. They wanted to find work and make a better life for themselves and their children. One factor that influenced the British government's decision to open its doors to the West Indies migrants was World War II. Britain had been badly bombed during the war and was in desperate need of workers. These migrants helped to rebuild the country.

It is easy to forget how difficult it was for the first immigrants from the Caribbean when they arrived. Not only was the climate completely different, but the society and culture was not always as welcoming as they had expected. They faced many difficulties as they tried to make a home in their new country.

Today, their children and grandchildren are an important part of Britain's multicultural society. They have changed the idea of what it means to be British.

▶ 7.2 What've you been doing?; How long've you been living here?; Where's she been staying?

▶ 7.3 **1.** How long will you be traveling?; **2.** What will you be studying?; **3.** Where have you been working?; **4.** Why have you been coming home late?

▶ 7.4 **1.** How long has he been living here?; **2.** How have you been feeling recently?; **3.** What has she been working on recently?; **4.** Where have they been studying?

▶ 7.5 Globalization and migration in the world today means that we are living in an increasingly multicultural world. But what does multiculturalism really mean?

Multiculturalism often refers to societies in which people from different ethnic backgrounds live together in one community. By this definition, some of the most ethnically diverse countries are in Africa. For example, Chad in north-central Africa is home to more than 100 ethnic groups. Uganda in east Africa is home to more than 40 different ethnic groups.

Another way of looking at multiculturalism is to look at the number of different languages spoken in a country. Singapore, for example, has four official languages: English, Mandarin Chinese, Malay, and Tamil. However, most people use English to communicate with each other. Another example is India, where Hindi and English are the official national languages. Each state also has its own official language.

But these versions of multiculturalism do not always look at the complex nature of what multiculturalism means. It doesn't include people who belong to more than one culture, or who don't define themselves by their ethnicity or their language. Do these different ethnic groups feel represented, recognized, and respected in their new culture? These are just some of the questions that can help us understand what it means for a society to be multicultural.

▶ **8.1** What's the best way to reduce traffic congestion, noise, and air pollution in cities? Encourage people to cycle more! But how do you do that? One increasingly popular idea is for cities to introduce bike-sharing program.

So what is a bike-sharing program and how does it work? The main concept is to provide bicycles that are available for public use. You borrow a bicycle in one place, ride to your destination, and return it to another place. This means that the bikes can be used by several users in one day.

Bike-share programs charge for their use in different ways. Users pay an annual fee or a daily fee for each ride. In London, for example, where there are 11,000 bikes and almost 600 bike stations. You can pay an annual fee of £90 or £4 per hour for a whole day's use. In Paris, there are over 23,000 bikes and 1,800 bike stations. The annual fee is €29. If you choose to pay the daily fee, it's free for the first half hour, but you pay a charge of between €1 and €4 for each half hour after that. In Hangzhou, China, bike-riders pay a deposit of 200 Chinese Yuan (about $33) and ride free of charge for the first hour. Each additional hour is then charged an extra 1 Chinese Yuan (about 15 cents). Currently, there are 60,000 bikes and 2,400 bike stations in Hangzhou, but the city plans to increase this number in the years to come.

▶ **8.2** **1.** In the future, most cars are going to run on electricity instead of gas.; **2.** I'm sure that there will be high-speed, long-distance trains underground. The technology is already available.; **3.** It will be a long time before many people can afford to travel to space.; **4.** Maybe air pollution will get better in the future.

▶ **8.3** I'll go to the moon for a holiday.; They'll invent a way to live longer.; I'll be able to travel in time.; Robots'll replace humans in the workplace.; Cars'll get faster and safer.; Cities'll get bigger and bigger.

▶ **8.4** **1.** We travel by car to work.; **2.** Neighborhoods will become more crowded.; **3.** We communicate via video chat.; **4.** Most people live in large cities.; **5.** Robots will do a variety of jobs.; **6.** I'll work remotely from home.

▶ **8.5** **1.** Do you think people in cities will have happier lives?; **2.** Do you think robots make our lives easier?; **3.** Do you think renewable energy sources will help to reduce pollution?

▶ **8.6** As our cities continue to grow, it's clear that the problem of traffic congestion and pollution is going to get worse. Many cities around the world are looking at ways to reduce the number of cars on the road and to improve the driving experience for road users.

One strategy that has worked in London is the introduction of a special fee for entering the city by car on weekdays. Called a "congestion charge," the fee applies to all types of road vehicles and must be paid before entering the city. Cars that have not paid the fee are captured on camera and fined. The scheme was first introduced in 2003. Ten years later, there was found to be a 10% reduction of traffic in the city center.

Another strategy to reduce the number of cars is the introduction of carpool lanes or HOV lanes (high occupancy vehicle lanes). These are special lanes on the highways than can only be used by drivers who have at least one passenger in their car. While the main lanes of the highway are crowded with cars containing only the driver, HOV lanes are often emptier and move faster.

Finally, in the future, our cars will definitely be "smart cars," that is, cars that are equipped with wireless technology. Eventually, smart cars and trucks will be able to form groups of 8, 10, or more vehicles—all electronically linked so they can closely follow each other without crashing. This system however, would require finding large numbers of cars that want to go to the same destination at the same time in order to be cost effective.

▶ **9.1** One of the first English dictionaries was written in 1775 by Samuel Johnson. Johnson examined many articles and identified the usage of specific words. Each example was written on a separate card. He based his definition on an analysis of all the examples. His great dictionary took nine years to create.

Since then, dictionaries have gone through many transformations. As the English language has evolved, and many new words are added to the language, other words fall out of use or change their meaning.

Today's dictionaries are compiled using very similar methods to those used by Samuel Johnson many years ago. The definitions are still based on real examples of how people use language. But the data sources today are far more extensive. It is possible to analyze the English used in written and spoken form by sampling the Internet, as well as newspapers, books, songs, films, and a lot more.

Another difference is that dictionaries today often include a lot of slang, regional, or non-standard words, as well as technical words. So they're even larger than ever before.

Dictionaries are constantly being updated. It used to take many years to update a dictionary, because they were all in print form. But now, with electronic versions available online, dictionaries can be updated far more quickly and easily.

▶ **9.2** People used to write letters and send postcards.; People used letters and postcards to keep in touch.; Phones didn't use to have cameras in them.; People didn't use their phones to take photos.

▶ **9.3** **1.** People used to invent different words for new ideas.; **2.** The same slang words are used among certain groups of people.; **3.** We didn't use to have so many ways of communicating.; **4.** My friends used to laugh at me because I didn't have a phone.; **5.** I used my friend's phone to call my parents.

▶ **9.4** **1.** What language did you use to study?; **2.** What are these apps used for?; **3.** What did people use to write about in their diaries?; **4.** What instrument did she use to play as a young girl?; **5.** What are these nanorobots used for?

▶ **9.5** **1.** Dictionaries used to be much smaller.; **2.** I used to use a print dictionary.; **3.** I use the Internet to look up new words.; **4.** Dictionaries didn't use to be updated so often.;
5. Did you use your dictionary to check the spelling?

▶ **9.6** Increasing globalization, the Internet and many other factors mean that we're all using more English words than ever before. Many see this as a natural way for languages to evolve, but for some it is seen as a threat to their national culture and identity.

One example is Iceland. Icelandic is an ancient language, dating back to the thirteenth and fourteenth centuries. But English is widely spoken as a second language in Iceland, and some worry that it will soon take over and their national language will disappear.

For this reason, the Icelandic government has set up an institute to protect the Icelandic language. The task of this institute is to monitor the use of English words in Icelandic and find alternative words for saying the same thing. And it's not only the institute that is preserving the language. Icelanders themselves have formed language committees to find modern usages for ancient words. For example, instead of using the word *telephone*, the institute borrowed the word *simi* from the ancient Icelandic word for *thread*. Another example is *myndband,* which means "video" or "picture band."

One advantage of this approach to language preservation is that standard Icelandic has changed very little over the last 300 years. Therefore, most Icelanders are able to read and understand ancient Icelandic. However, although there are those who believe that the best way to preserve the Icelandic language is to resist change, there are others who believe that a language has to evolve and develop in order to stay alive.

▶ 10.1

M: You're looking a bit down today—is something wrong?

W: I'm having a problem at work. It's the manager of our department. She's making life really difficult for me.

M: What do you mean?

W: Well, she's always giving me extra work, much more than the others, and whenever she speaks to me she's just really rude and it makes me so upset!

M: Oh no, that's really insensitive of her. Have you tried talking to her about it?

W: No, but I talked to someone else in the department and they said she did the same thing to someone else in her previous job.

M: Oh I see. Well, that seems like it's something to do with her personality then, doesn't it? It's nothing to do with you. You really mustn't take it so personally. In my opinion, the best thing for you to do would be to talk to her about it. If that doesn't work, then you could talk to someone higher up.

W: I don't know … I'm afraid that might make it worse.

M: Well, if it's upsetting you this much, you really need to do something about it.

▶ 10.2 **1.** I'm going for an interview on Monday.; **2.** Don't forget to do your homework.; **3.** I can't understand what you're saying.; **4.** I'll pick you up at 7 p.m.

▶ 10.3 She said she'd apply for another job. She said she'd applied for another job.

▶ 10.4 **1.** Did Martin say he'd sent in his application?; **2.** Did they ask if you'd lived overseas?; **3.** Did you say you'd worked as a manager?; **4.** He said he'd studied Biology.; **5.** She asked if he'd picked up the shopping items.

▶ 10.5 **1.** Did you say you'd traveled to Paris?; **2.** Did Wendy say she'd apply for the position?; **3.** Did he say he'd lived in China?; **4.** Did she say she'd join the soccer team?

▶ 10.6 Technology that tells others how you're feeling? Is it good or is it bad? We all know about wearable technology that tracks our physical activity and our heart rate, but what about technology that tracks our emotions or our moods?

At first glance, this seems like such a great idea! Just imagine the effect it would have on business meetings or staff meetings! No need to ask if someone is angry or upset—and if stress levels get too high—you'll know when it's time for a coffee break! Sounds good, doesn't it?

But wait a minute. Let's just ask how this technology tracks our emotions. It does this by measuring our physical state—pulse rate, breathing rate, temperature, sweat and so on. This is one way to measure stress levels, but these are all still just physical indications. They don't present a complete picture of our internal emotions. Emotions are far more complex than just the four or five states that these devices can measure. We can experience joy, sadness, anger or calm, but also endless combinations of these emotions and so many others as well!

Another point to consider is whether we really want other people to know how we're feeling. It's fine and probably very useful for people to be aware of their own stress levels, but do I really want my boss or co-worker to know that I'm angry or fed up—it might not help our relationship at all! And could in fact have the opposite effect. When it comes to our feelings, privacy is a very important aspect of our communication system. Let's face it, there are some things that we'd just really prefer not to share!

▶ 11.1 Are you thinking about starting a business online? But how easy is it really? Here are some easy tips for starting your own online business.

The first thing to do is to identify your market and find out exactly what kind of product is not available. Let's say, for example, that you are interested in creating toys for pets. Try visiting popular blogs and online forums, read reviews to find out what people are looking for and why they aren't satisfied with the products that are already available. Once you have identified a gap in the market, you can create a product that will help fill that gap.

The next thing to do is to create your website. There are plenty of companies out there that will design one for you, but you need to know what you really want. What kind of image do you want to project and what kind of functions and features do you need to have? Write a description of your products that is catchy and appealing and create attractive photos and graphics to go with it.

Finally, think about ways to market your products. One way is to become an active contributor to social networking sites and social forums. You might give advice on taking care of cats, for example. Then include a link to your website. If people like your article, they will be likely to visit your site.

▶ **11.2** **1.** Teachers should encourage students to voice their own opinions in class.; **2.** If you want to succeed, you mustn't give up when things get tough.; **3.** All staff have to wear formal clothing.; **4.** You shouldn't be afraid of making mistakes.; **5.** I need to pick up the kids from school at 3:30.

▶ **11.3** You must be able to recruit the right people.; We should meet for coffee and discuss the plan.; Do I have to work this weekend?; Things may not go according to plan.

▶ **11.4** **1.** You shouldn't be afraid of taking risks.; **2.** Even if the odds are against you, you should do it.; **3.** Leaders need to inspire people.; **4.** You need to be ambitious.; **5.** People with no experience of business may find it hard.; **6.** You only realize your mistakes afterwards.

▶ **11.5** **1.** the end; **2.** too often; **3.** you all; **4.** lie on; **5.** the arcade

▶ **11.6** Most people are afraid of failure. We all want to be a success and are embarrassed by our mistakes. But like most things in life, the process of learning involves making mistakes and failing in one way or another. It's the way we learn from our mistakes that helps us to turn these failures into successes. Here is some advice on how to learn from failure.

If an idea isn't working, you need to find ways of adjusting and refining it so that it works. In business for example, getting market feedback on products and testing them out can inspire you to refine your idea, instead of abandoning it and giving up.

On the other hand, you should also recognize when an idea really isn't working. When you've invested a lot of time and money in an idea, it's hard to give up and try something new. But sometimes that is exactly what you have to do. If an idea doesn't work, you mustn't be afraid to go back to the drawing board and start from scratch.

Have confidence in yourself! Your ideas may be turned down hundreds of times, but if you believe in what you're doing and think it is worthwhile, don't give up, just keep trying.

Make the most of your unique qualities. Although others may criticize them, you can turn them into strengths. You don't need to be defined by others' opinions, as long you know what your strengths are and how to apply them.

▶ **12.1** A lot of people have trouble falling asleep or wake up frequently during the night. If this condition continues for a long period of time, it is known as insomnia. Insomnia affects many people, but research suggests it becomes more common as we get older. People over 65 are the most likely to suffer from insomnia.

The causes of insomnia can vary from person to person. It is sometimes caused by lifestyle factors. Too much caffeine, for example, can definitely keep you awake, as caffeine stays in your system for up to eight hours. Eating meals late at night or eating spicy foods in the evening can also disrupt your sleep.

Technology is also thought to be a cause of insomnia. Researchers found that children with TVs and computers in their bedrooms slept far less than children without them. So if you're reading your phone messages or emails late at night, that could be why you're having difficulty falling asleep.

One of the most common reasons for lack of sleep is worry or stress. You might start thinking about problems just as you're trying to fall asleep, or wake up during the night and start thinking about them. A stressful job, a relationship problem, or financial problems can often seem so overwhelming that it prevents you from going back to sleep.

Occasional lack of sleep is quite normal, but If insomnia starts to become a regular pattern, then it's important to identify the cause so that you can change your lifestyle. You can develop new habits that enable you to get the sleep you need so that you are able to recharge your batteries and be more productive in your daily life.

▶ **12.2** **1.** If I had $3 million, I'd donate it to charity.; **2.** If she were rich, she'd travel the world.; **3.** If I lived by the sea, I'd go surfing every week.; **4.** If I were you, I'd look for a new place to live.

▶ 12.3 What will you do with the money?; What would you do with the money?; I think I'll spend it on a new car.; I think I'd spend it on a new car.

▶ 12.4 **1.** How would you feel?; **2.** Where do you think you'll go?; **3.** I'll probably take the train.; **4.** I'd be really surprised.; **5.** He'll be a great manager.; **6.** It'll cost about a million dollars.; **7.** I think she'd be really upset.; **8.** Do you think it'd work?

▶ 12.5 **1.** What would you buy if you won the lottery?; **2.** Do you think he'll come if we invite him?; **3.** I'll be late if I don't hurry.; **4.** I'd apologize if I were you.; **5.** Do you think he'd lend me some money?

▶ 12.6 Many countries in the world have a work culture that involves working long hours and doing overtime—sometimes even on weekends. This make it very difficult to achieve a good work-life balance.

Two countries where people are expected to work very long hours are Singapore and South Korea. Singaporeans typically work 46 hours per week, according to a Singstat report for 2014. In South Korea, it is even longer—an average of 47 hours. The result? Fewer people are starting families. Parents who work such long hours have very little time or energy left to spend with their children, not to mention the difficulty and expense of arranging childcare or care for children when they are sick.

However, these countries are looking towards Denmark, where the government offers many incentives to help parents spend time with their children. Workers in Denmark work an average of 33 hours a week. They can work from home and can leave work at 3pm to pick up their children from childcare. That gives them plenty of time to play and read and spend time with their children.

Changing the work culture isn't easy. Many companies in Singapore and South Korea still value the ability to closely monitor workers in the office. They don't trust workers to get their work done at home, even though some studies have shown that working from home can increase productivity as there are fewer distractions. That is something that may change if employers start to actively support parents and encourage a good work-life balance.

Credits

Photo Credits

Cover Gerd Ludwig/National Geographic Creative, **3** Kevork Djansezian/Getty Images News/Getty Images, **9** Theo Wargo/Getty Images Entertainment/Getty Images, **11** Design Pics Inc/National Geographic Creative, **12** The Asahi Shimbun/The Asahi Shimbun/Getty Images, **17** Ari Perilstein/Getty Images Entertainment/Getty Images, **19** Westend61 GmbH/Alamy Stock Photo, **20** George Leroy/Alamy Stock Photo, **25** RioPatuca/Alamy Stock Photo, **27** BSIP/Newscom, **28** Chris So/Toronto Star/Getty Images, **32** (tl) Future Music Magazine/Future/Getty Images, (tc) Maksym Bondarchuk/Shutterstock.com, (tr) Peter Kotoff/Shutterstock.com, **33** Kaspars Grinvalds/Shutterstock.com, **35** Westend61/Getty Images, **36** Bloomberg/Getty Images, **41** © Bruno Ruganzu Tusingwire, **44** Alison Hancock/Shutterstock.com, **49** © Maddalena Bearzi, **51** Tomasz Bidermann/Shutterstock.com, **52** David Parker & Julian Baum/Science Source, **57** Alexander Image/Shutterstock.com, **60** © James Duncan Davidson/TED, **65** AP Images/Andy Wong, **68** B.S.P.I./Corbis Documentary/Getty Images, **73** (tr) Photographee.eu/Shutterstock.com, (cr) Thomas Barwick/DigitalVision/Getty Images, (br) Bloomberg/Getty Images, **76** B Christopher/Alamy Stock Photo, **81** Bloomberg/Getty Images, **84** Anadolu Agency/Getty Images, **89** (tr) DPA Picture Alliance/Alamy Stock Photo, (cr) John Lamparski/WireImage/Getty Images, (br) King World Productions/Everett Collection, **92** Ezra Bailey/Taxi/Getty Images, **97** Edgardo Contreras/Taxi/Getty Images, **100** Image Source Salsa/Alamy Stock Photo

Text Credits

49 Adapted from “5 Simple Tips for Communicating Science”: voice.nationalgeographic.com, October 2013